On Your Knees!

ON YOUR KNEES!
St. Paul at Prayer

Michael Green

eagle

Eagle
Guildford, Surrey

Copyright © 1992 Michael Green

ISBN No: 0 86347 085 8

British Library Cataloguing-in-Publication Data. A catalogue
record for this book is available from the British Library.

Published by Eagle, an imprint of Inter Publishing Service (IPS)
Ltd, Williams Building, Woodbridge Meadows, Guildford, Surrey
GU1 1BH.

Typeset by Falcon Typographic Art Ltd,
Fife, Scotland
Printed in the UK by
HarperCollins Manufacturing, Glasgow.

**Dedicated to my prayer partners
far and wide**

Contents

The God to Whom Paul Prayed

1

The God to Whom
Paul Prayed

We shall be looking in some detail in this book at
the prayers which the apostle Paul allows us to
overhear – for they are written in his letters which
form part of our Bible. But who did he think he was
praying to? What God did he believe in, this Jewish
Pharisee who was once such a passionate persecutor of the Christians, and then became their most
powerful ambassador? It's an important question.

Nearly everyone believes in a God of some sort:
some force which set the world going, if nothing
more than that. Well, that was not the God to
whom Paul prayed. Many people see god as so far
removed from us that he could not possibly know or
care about mere mortals like us. That was not the
God to whom Paul prayed. An increasing number
of people these days identify God with the natural
world in which we live, and see the mountains and
seas, the flowers and birds, and above all ourselves,

as divine. That was not the God to whom Paul prayed.

Paul's God was much greater and more wonderful than any of those understandings of him. Paul, both in his days as a Jew and his days as a Christian, was a passionate believer in personal, ethical monotheism.

Monotheism – God is the single ultimate source of everything in the universe.

Personal – There is no doubt that God is beyond personality, but he is *at least* personal, since he is the Creator of persons like ourselves.

Ethical – He cares deeply about right and wrong: he is the moral ruler of the universe.

That is the God in whom Paul believed, and to whom he prayed. He was confident that this God was *transcendent* – beyond our world of space and time, and was also *immanent* – within every flower and person and sunset: beyond us, but alongside us. He is the God who has the power to act, because he is so great, and the God who utterly understands, because he is intimately involved in the world he made and the people within it.

I suppose we could set it out like this. Here are eight aspects of the God to whom Paul prays. They come out clearly in his writings.

The God who creates

Paul is convinced that God is the creator of the universe, and that all who do not deliberately suppress that knowledge are aware of the fact. 'Since what may be known about God is plain to them, because God has made it plain to them. For since the creation of the world God's invisible qualities – his eternal power and divine nature – have been clearly seen, being understood from what has been made' (Romans 1:19,20).

The God who reveals

'From infancy', he writes to his young lieutenant Timothy, 'you have known the holy Scriptures, which are able to make you wise for salvation through faith in Christ Jesus. All Scripture is God-breathed and is useful for teaching, rebuking, correcting and training in righteousness, so that the man of God may be thoroughly equipped for every good work' (2 Timothy 3:15,16). We are not left to grope after God in the dark. He has shown his hand.

The God of Israel

Paul's God was not newly invented. He is the God of Abraham, of Isaac and of Jacob, the God worshipped and adored by the Jewish people. Paul never goes back on that conviction. He says of Israel and her God, 'The people of Israel. Theirs is the

13

adoption as sons; theirs the divine glory, the covenants, the receiving of the law, the temple worship and the promises. Theirs are the patriarchs, and from them is traced the human ancestry of Christ, who is God over all, for ever praised!' (Romans 9:4–5). It is this profound sense of continuity with all that God had done in Israel which allows him to congratulate Christians, of mixed Jewish and Gentile stock, for being descendants of Abraham. 'You are all one in Christ Jesus. If you belong to Christ, then you are Abraham's seed, and heirs according to the promise' (Galatians 3:28–29).

The God who came in Christ

The God Paul worships is no careless absentee who set the world going and then lost interest in it. Although, as Paul puts it, men 'did not think it worth while to retain the knowledge of God' (Romans 1:28), God came to find us. He came as a man among men. His name was Jesus. 'Who, being in very nature God, did not consider equality with God something to be grasped, but made himself nothing, . . . being made in human likeness. And being found in appearance as a man, he humbled himself and became obedient to death – even death on a cross!' (Philippians 2:6–8). That is how much God cares for us. That is what he is prepared to endure for us. No wonder Paul found it a joy to pray to such a God with confidence.

14

The God who saves

Why did God bother to come and seek us? In order to rescue us from the predicament, the fatal predicament, into which our race had fallen by our stupid self-centredness. We rested under the 'curse' of his judgment, and to Paul's endless wonder 'Christ redeemed us from the curse of the [broken] law by becoming a curse for us' (Galatians 3:13). He spells it out a little some verses later. 'But when the time had fully come, God sent his Son, born of a woman, born under the law, to redeem those under the law, that we might receive the full rights of sons' (Galatians 4:4–5). Yes, 'there is one God and one mediator between God and men, the man Christ Jesus, who gave himself as a ransom for all men' (1 Timothy 2:5). Consequently Paul could come with utter confidence to God in prayer, knowing he was accepted because of Christ. 'Therefore, since we have been justified through faith, we have peace with God through our Lord Jesus Christ, through whom we have gained access' (Romans 5:1–2).

The God who indwells

Paul is fundamentally confident, because this God is not far off, not extinguished on the cross, but alive in the hearts of believers. 'If the Spirit of him who raised Jesus from the dead is living in you, he who raised Christ from the dead will also give life to your mortal bodies through his Spirit, who lives in you' (Romans 8:11). That fundamentally affects his prayer life. 'And by him we cry, "*Abba*, Father." The Spirit himself testifies with our spirit that we are God's children. Now if children, then we are heirs . . .' (Romans 8:15–17). Indeed, the Spirit is that part of the Godhead who lives in believers and helps them to pray. 'In the same way, the Spirit helps us in our weakness. We do not know what we ought to pray for, but the Spirit himself intercedes for us with groans that words cannot express. And he who searches our hearts knows the mind of the Spirit, because the Spirit intercedes for the saints in accordance with God's will' (Romans 8:26–27).

The God who judges

Paul is very aware that God remains Judge in his world. 'God . . . who will judge the living and the dead'; he looks to the day when 'God will judge men's secrets through Jesus Christ' (2 Timothy 4:1, Romans 2:16). And although the Christian is accepted in Christ and will not finally be lost, there remains a day of reckoning for Christians too. 'For we must all appear before the judgment seat of Christ' (2 Corinthians 5:10). This keeps the apostle humble and serious in his prayers. He never takes the mercy of God for granted.

The God who awaits

The final glory of the gospel lies in just this: God will never scrap what is precious to him – and his people

16

are very precious: he died to win their love. So at the end of the road there is the waiting Father. 'Now there is in store for me the crown of righteousness, which the Lord, the righteous Judge, will award to me on that day – and not only to me, but also to all who have longed for his appearing' (2 Timothy 4:8). That gives him enormous joy in his life and in his prayers. 'For I am convinced that neither death nor life, neither angels nor demons, neither the present nor the future, nor any powers, neither height nor depth, nor anything else in all creation, will be able to separate us from the love of God that is in Christ Jesus our Lord' (Romans 8:38–39).

If that is the sort of God you believe in, it gives you enormous confidence to pray, does it not? It certainly did to Paul.

An Example for Us?

2

An Example for Us?

Prayer! It does not come easily to us, does it? Almost everyone prays, atheists included, at times of stress and danger. But few of us, Christians included, have an ease, an intimacy in prayer such as you would expect to find in family conversation between children and parents. This is an area where, above almost anywhere else in the spiritual life, we need help.

And God in his generosity has provided it. He has given us a model in prayer. 'Oh', you say, 'Some saint, some monk, insulated from the pressures of normal life? Someone who doesn't understand the strains and stresses I have to face?' Not at all. In Saul of Tarsus, the persecutor who became the apostle Paul, God has given us someone who can help us enormously in this matter of prayer.

It did not come easily to him, either. Paul was an activist – and activists are notoriously weak at relaxed, meditative prayer.

Paul was quick tempered and critical – hardly the soil in which to grow the gentle plant of prayer.

Paul was an intellectual of the highest stature – with all the intellectual's determination to think his way through a problem, rather than pray his way through.

And Paul was proud. Proud of his nationality, his religion, his background, his wealth, his rectitude, his competence. People like that find prayer very difficult. They often have to be broken first. Paul had to be, on the Damascus Road. You see, pride says 'My will be done', and prayer says 'Thy will be done'. The two are miles apart.

No, we may be sure that prayer did not come easily to this fiery intellectual. Yet God in his goodness used precisely such a man, with all his faults, facing all these pressures, to be a model to Christians in the matter of prayer. Had he chosen one of the desert fathers, one of the medieval mystics, one of the gentle meditative spirits that have from time to time graced the Christian community, I could have understood it. Instead, he chose this most unlikely man, as if to tell us that intellect need be no barrier to prayer. Activity need be no barrier to prayer. Temperament need be no barrier to prayer. A life on the road need be no barrier to prayer. Organisational skills need not be incompatible with a deep life of prayer: they are, in fact, disastrous without it.

An Example for Us?

Saul of Tarsus shows us that whatever our temperament, our job, our skills, our weaknesses, God can make us men and women of prayer. I am so grateful for that. There is hope for the likes of you and me!

Through a Friend's Eyes

3

Through a Friend's Eyes

What an embarrassing place to start! How intimate. We do not like to reveal our prayer life to
somebody else. To be sure, we will talk about prayer
until the cows come home. We will cheerfully join
in public prayer in church, or pray informally in
the Prayer Meeting, perhaps; but to allow our own
practice of private prayer to be observed by someone
else is a rather different matter. What if they discovered how barren and empty I am feeling, inside
the cheery outer appearance? What if they found
out how rarely I pray, and how perfunctory it often
is? No, I would not like to have my personal prayer
life examined, even by a close and understanding
friend. But Paul's prayer life was scrutinised in this
way. And, to me at least, his friend's testimony to
Paul's prayer life is even more impressive than the
references to it which the apostle himself makes
– because it is someone else looking in, someone
who could not be taken in by externals, someone

who knew Paul intimately. That friend was Luke. Luke the doctor, Luke the companion of St Paul on many of his journeys, Luke who went through the rigours of prison with him and the hazards of shipwreck. Now Luke does not set out in the Acts of the Apostles to write about the prayer life of his friend. But he does let slip a number of allusions which show us that he noticed it, and that he was moved by it. So let us come alongside Luke, and catch some glimpses of Paul at prayer, through the eyes of his friend. Five things at least jump out of the pages of the Acts on the subject of Paul's prayers.

Prayer was the sign of life

There is a very remarkable little phrase in the story of St Paul's conversion. Ananias is told by God to go and visit Saul of Tarsus, this fearsome enemy of the budding Christian movement. He can go without trepidation to that house in Straight Street to ask for Saul, 'for he is praying' (Acts 9:11). Just that, but what an eloquent phrase. It reveals so much. And it is perfectly astonishing. You see, the Jew's life was bathed in prayer. His orthodox Jewish parents would have conceived Saul in prayer, have brought him to birth in prayer. His earliest memories would be prayers with his mother, Friday night prayers in the home, synagogue prayers on the sabbath, temple prayers on great festal occasions. Orthodox Jews would pray before any substantial talk or enjoyment. There would be prayers at three fixed times in the day (Psalm 55:17). As a Pharisee Saul would have laid special emphasis on prayer. He would have worn the prayer shawl, prayed publicly and out loud as befitted a Pharisee, a 'separated one' (Matt. 6:5).

And yet he had not begun to pray! He simply said prayers. And did those prayers reach God? The Pharisee in Jesus' story, you may remember, 'prayed *about himself*' (Luke 18:11). It was only when, like the 'publican' he cried 'God, have mercy on me, a sinner' on the road to Damascus, that he really got through to God for the first time in his life. For prayer is communion with God, and nothing hinders it so much as the proud, sinful self-centredness which is such a characteristic of us all. It comes like a cloud between us and the sun. And it is only when we are humble enough to come to God for his pardon that the cloud rolls away, and the light and the warmth of his sunshine begin to become real to us. In other words, prayer is the fruit of getting on the right terms with God.

A story is told of Admiral Nelson after one of his victories over the French fleet. The opposing

admiral came onto his quarter-deck and offered
Nelson his hand. 'Your sword first, sir' said Nelson.
There could be no companionship until there had
been explicit surrender. And that is what Paul
did at his conversion. He gave in to God. He
admitted that God was in the right and he was
not. His proud knees bowed, and he cried to God
for mercy. That is when prayer first became real
to him.

Interestingly enough, Paul himself later described
prayer as the firstfruit of reconciliation with God
in that famous passage in Romans 5:1 where he
writes:

'Therefore, since we have been justified through
faith, we have peace with God through our Lord
Jesus Christ, through whom we have gained
access . . .'

That is it, access! The barriers are down and
access is available. That is a lovely way to think
of prayer, access. Whereas in the past there was a
forbidding notice 'No Through Road', we now read
the encouraging sign 'Way clear'.

Let the wonder of this touch us afresh. We have
turned away from God – yes? Well, 'if anyone
turns a deaf ear to the law, even his prayers are
detestable' (Prov. 28:9, and *cf.* Isa. 1:15; Psalm

66:18). But in the wonder of the good news, God, as Karl Barth so charmingly put it, 'invites us to live with him'.

Prayer, real prayer, is the first sign of new life with God. It is interesting, and no doubt auto-biographical, that when Paul in Galatians 4:4–7 briefly sketches the story of salvation, he makes the believer's cry of 'Abba, dear Father' the crowning evidence of sonship. It is the assurance that we belong in the family. Just as the first sign of life in a new baby when it is born into the world is a cry, so the first sign of life when we are born anew into God's family is a cry, a prayer. God has no dumb children. They always begin to speak to him in prayer.

Of course, we can say prayers without being in the family of God. We can recite liturgy, we can go to church, we can sit in prayer meetings, or stand in revival meetings with glazed eyes and arms in the air. But real prayer is a sign of life, an early demonstration that the Spirit of God has taken up residence and is beginning to enliven our spirit. It is perhaps the most important sign of spiritual life, just as breathing is of physical life. At all events, it is the only sign God gave to Ananias of Saul's change of heart.

If our own lives were judged by that same criterion, could we hold our heads high? 'He is praying.' Are we? Maybe we are alive by that standard,

but how healthy are we? Let us put the thermom-
eter of prayer under our tongue and quietly take
the reading. It is an uncomfortably accurate guide
to spiritual health.

Prayer was the means of guidance

Let us stay with Saul for a few moments longer in
that house in Straight Street, Damascus. There is
more to learn from that tantalisingly brief reference. It not only shows us that prayer was the sign
of life, but also that prayer was the means of God's
guidance in Saul's life. For what does it say? 'In a
vision he has seen a man named Ananias come and
place his hands on him to restore his sight.' Imagine
this proud, intellectual, zealous Pharisee, so used
to commanding, and to leading, for the first time
ever reduced to total immobility. For three days,
we read, he was blind after the Damascus Road
experience, and no food or water passed his lips.
Just imagine it! Three days without food is more
than most of us could readily face. But three days
in total blindness, not knowing whether you will
ever see again, three days without food or drink –
that must have been a terrifying experience. And
it took all of that to bring Saul to a place where he
would listen to God and seek his direction and his

plan. It was during this terrible time that Saul was still for long enough to receive God's guidance. And that guidance was very specific. Saul was shown that release was at hand. He was shown the very name of the person who would bring it. He was shown the method that would be used to restore his sight. Amazing! And God showed it all to him as he prayed. He could never have imagined those things – and got them right. He could never have planned them with his organisational skills. God showed him, once he was brought to the point of inner stillness and dependence.

I think of a couple who used to be in the same church as me. They were accustomed to waiting on God in prayer. The husband's job changed, and he needed to take his little family to another part of the country. As they contemplated the move, his wife, Sue, had a vision of the house they would live in. It had definite and unusual features. Well, they went to see the town where the new job lay. They spent a whole day going round houses that were for sale, and found nothing that seemed suitable, let alone resembling the picture which the wife had had. On their last morning they saw a few more houses, again without success. Suddenly, they saw the very house of which Sue had received a picture. There was no 'For sale' sign outside. But still, they prevailed on the estate agent to let them go and knock on the door. They did – and you can guess the sequel. The owners said 'As a matter of fact we have put this house on the market today, but no signs are up as yet.' The price was far too high. So my friends offered what they could – and waited. In due course, other potential buyers all fell by the wayside, and my friends bought it at the price they could afford, and are happily ensconced in it today and using it for ministry to other people. God gave very specific guidance in this instance as they waited on him in prayer. The God who guided Saul specifically is still in business!

The Acts of the Apostles gives us two other clear examples of the apostle being guided as he prayed. One is in chapter 22:17–18. Paul is alone in the temple, praying. Again we see the true nature of prayer, communion with God.

'When I . . . was praying at the temple, I fell into a trance and saw the Lord speaking. "Quick!" he said to me. "Leave Jerusalem immediately, because they will not accept your testimony about me."'

A very instructive passage. Paul the great man of action is Paul the great man of prayer. His talking about God is matched by his talking to God.

On this occasion he loses all account of time: he is face to face with the Eternal. As he prays, God makes his will clear to him. The warning saved Paul's life. We do not know if Paul was asking about his future. At all events, a humble, receptive attitude to God in prayer made it easy for the Lord to get through to him with something Paul very much needed to hear! He was willing to obey God, cost what it might. He prayed. And God guided him.

Do you want guidance about your future, your job perhaps? Well, we may reverently say that it is God's job to guide you: it is your job to seek his will in an attitude of openness and obedience. He does not tell us *how* he may make his will known to us, but he *does* undertake to do it. 'He guides the humble in what is right and teaches them his way' (Psalm 25:9). We should not pray 'Bless my way, O Lord' but rather 'Teach me your way, O Lord' (Psalm 27:11).

A third example of God guiding Paul's life through prayer comes in Acts chapter 13. The scene has changed dramatically. From the Jewish temple service we move to the Gentile church meeting. No longer alone, Paul is in company. He was in the midst of one of the most remarkable churches in the ancient world, the church at Antioch. This church, founded by wandering laymen, became the springboard of world mission.

'In the church at Antioch there were prophets and teachers: Barnabas, Simeon called Niger,

Lucius of Cyrene, Manaen (who had been brought up with Herod the tetrarch) and Saul. While they were worshipping the Lord and fasting, the Holy Spirit said, "Set apart for me Barnabas and Saul for the work to which I have called them." So after they had fasted and prayed, they placed their hands on them and sent them off.' (Acts 13:1–3)

There was real fellowship there – no pride of place: five men are mentioned as forming the corporate leadership of that church, and Paul is mentioned last in the list. There was no social distinction there: the group contained one black man and one member of the ruling *élite*! And they were all intent on one thing – God's glory. They were 'worshipping' him: the word used in the Greek suggests something much more formal than the private prayer of chapter 22. Do not despise public, formal prayer: enter into it, and learn to use it. God can well make his way known through it.

Moreover these Antioch Christians fasted. This is a vital accessory to serious prayer. It tells God that we love him more, even, than food. It tells him we mean business about prayer. We should not have a narrow view of fasting, as if it was always a matter of doing without a meal or two. No, fasting may mean temporary abstinence from sleep, or sex, or sport, or T.V. It was when they fasted that God led them as a group to this new venture which would bring the gospel of Jesus out of the Jewish ghetto and into the Gentile world. God made it plain to them that they should release their two most gifted leaders to do overseas work.

What a contrast all this is to the modern church. How poverty-stricken our fellowship, how weak our prayer and fasting! As a result, how uncertain we usually are of the guidance of God, and how slow to take up imaginative initiatives. Prayer is the condition, the supreme condition – indeed, almost the only condition of guidance. God undertakes to guide us, but only if we really seek to discover and then to cooperate with his will.

I know something of that from personal experience. When wondering whether to accept a job at Regent College, Vancouver, for which there was no available finance, I found myself speaking to about 70 people in a hotel. I talked about the need for someone to teach evangelism at Regent College, but I resisted the idea that it should be me. As people left, one of them came up and said 'I will pay your salary'. I replied, in amazement, that it was not a question of 'me' but that he should go and make his offer known to the principal. He was followed by a lady who said 'I had a picture yesterday as I was praying with a friend. It was of a grand piano. I sensed that the lovely music coming from it was the music of the gospel. The piano was open, so that it masked the face of the person playing it. Behind it was a plate glass window. The room was large: I did not recognise it. After this picture my friend and I happened to pray for you; you were one among 18 people we were praying for that day. But having come to this reception today, I at once recognised the room. There was the plate glass window. There was the piano. You tried to sit at another table, but the principal uprooted you and put you at a table with him, just in front of the grand piano. And when you got up to speak, you declined to use the podium at the other end of the room, but spoke from just in front of the piano. I believe you are meant to come to Vancouver, and to spread the harmony of the gospel in evangelism.'

Well, I came, and it has been happening! That was a remarkable example of God directing my future through a vision received in prayer. I fought it for a year before I gave in. And how glad I am that I did give in. For the will of God is the best thing that could possibly happen to us, hard though we may find that to believe at any particular time of change in our lives!

Prayer was the secret of power

'Paul and Barnabas appointed elders for them in each church and, with prayer and fasting, committed them to the Lord . . .' (Acts 14:23)

Imagine the scene, in the wilds of Turkey, on that first memorable missionary journey out of Antioch. The gospel is proclaimed. The missionaries are kicked out of town, after provoking a riot with the Jews. Some of the hearers believe, particularly the fringe which had gathered around the synagogue. Others rejected the message. So what do Paul and Barnabas do? They ordain rivals to the synagogue leadership, and then disappear! It happened, apparently, 'in each church'. In that case I am not at all surprised to read verse 22. It is, in fact, an understatement that 'we must go through many hardships to enter the kingdom of God'.

Would you have liked to be in the shoes of one of these fledgling elders? I wonder what kept them spiritually alive? They had no senior minister to guide them, no church order or precedent to follow, no New Testament to read, no church buildings and no money. How did they manage to stand upright? Prayer. That is how. God strengthens us as we pray. That is, surely, why Paul begs again and again throughout his letters, 'Brothers, pray for us'.

Prayer is God's appointed channel for pouring his blessing on others. Some missionaries in foreign fields, some Christian friends in tough jobs are more strengthened by our prayers or harmed by the lack of them than we shall ever know. Some of my friends who have passed through various crises have been aware of a barrage of prayer for them just when they needed it most. It has lifted them – understandably.

But this is an area where we in the West are weak. Rationalistic children of the Enlightenment that we are, we are convinced at gut level that it is our intellect rather than our prayers that is critical for success in life. The churches believe this, with an accent on programme rather than on prayer. The theological colleges believe this, with an accent on theory rather than on prayer. The ordinary everyday Christian believes this, with only a very few moments spent in prayer each day. This shows where our priorities lie. We do not have because we do not ask, as James put it succinctly in his letter (James 4:2). Is it any wonder that we see so little of the power of God, compared with our prayer-conscious brothers and sisters in Korea and Singapore, in Sao Paulo and Dar es Salaam? They know that prayer is the pathway to power. And we, frankly, do not believe it.

Of course, it is not only for others that prayer is the key to effective, fruitful Christian living – though I mention others first because we are not naturally prone to forget ourselves! But remember Acts 16:25. It was as Paul and Silas sang praises and doubtless uttered heartfelt prayers in the filthy Philippian prison where they were incarcerated, that the earthquake took place which broke them free from their chains. Prayer was the gateway for release, and so it still is. I am sure the Philippians never forgot this amazing incident. Nor did Paul. When once again in prison, he writes to the Philippians, 'Yes, and I will continue to rejoice, for I know that through your prayers and the help given by the Spirit of Jesus Christ, what has happened to me will turn out for my deliverance' (Phil. 1:18*f.*). Paul knew, and his readers knew, that we are dealing with the God of the impossible. Prayer is the secret weapon at our disposal: it brings down into our experience the liberating power of Almighty God. In some mysterious way the 'help given by the Spirit of Jesus Christ' is linked with 'your prayers'.

Each one of us can think of some personal incidents of this kind, when we have known the power of prayer in our own lives and seen its manifest results. On a broader canvas, we have been privileged to see, in the space of one year, one of the most astonishing political reversals in all history, when the communist grip on Eastern Europe was broken in a few weeks: country followed country like a pack of cards falling to the table, as popular movements, in each case inspired by prayerful Christian believers, pioneered the path to freedom. I have never in my life witnessed such a breathtaking answer to prayer on such a massive scale. On the other hand, I wonder how much I personally, and the Christian Church corporately, have missed God's will and failed to experience his power, simply because we did not bother to do the one thing needful: to pray.

Prayer was the avenue for healing

'Publius, the chief official of the island, welcomed us to his home and for three days entertained us hospitably. His father was sick in bed, suffering from fever and dysentery. Paul went in to see him and, after prayer, placed his hands on him and healed him.' (Acts 28:7–8)

In the days of the New Testament, prayer, with or without the laying on of hands, with or without an anointing with oil (James 5:15), was a medium through which God was pleased to bring healing. It still is, all over the world. Though initially sceptical that God would intervene to answer prayer for physical healing, I have seen so much of it in my own ministry that I can only marvel at my earlier obtuseness and unbelief.

There are, however, two dangers we must avoid. Christian healing is a far cry from magic. It is not dependent on the right guru being present with the right formula. It is determined by the specific purpose of God, the God who knows what is best for all concerned (especially the sick person) in each individual situation. He generally discloses his will to some sensitive Christian present at such a time, which enables prayer to be offered with faith and deep confidence that we are praying according to his express will.

We must beware, however, of making exaggerated claims. God does not always heal when prayer is made – for reasons best known to himself. We must remember that we live in a fallen world, where God does not eradicate all sin any more than he eradicates all suffering. But in answer to prayer he can and does intervene, and give us a foretaste of the glory that shall be hereafter, when neither sin nor suffering will mar his creation. For now, it is salutary to recall, the same Paul who healed Publius' father had to leave his friend Trophimus at Miletus sick (2 Tim. 4:20). Indeed, he himself had to suffer agonies from some 'thorn in the flesh' for which he received the Lord's strengthening – but not his healing (2 Cor. 12:8–9).

But if we must beware of Christian triumphalism, which often adds insult to injury by maintaining that, if someone is not healed after prayer, this must be due either to their hidden sin or their lack of faith, we must no less beware of Christian rationalism and scepticism. Western man in general, often followed by the church in particular, is prone to turn to God in prayer for healing only as a last resort when all hope is gone. 'I'm so sorry', we say. 'The case seems hopeless, so perhaps we had better pray.' God should never be sought as a last resort. We should come to him first and foremost, before ever we turn to the doctor, and put our situation in his hands and seek his purposes for us. God is the God of salvation, and if you study that word in the scriptures you will find that time and again it embraces (indeed, very often actually *means*) healing. The church needs to become once again the healing community. For it is a sick and broken world out there, with sick bodies, sick minds, sick experiences, sick relationships, sick addictions. It cries out loud for the healing at many levels which only God can bring, and which he has determined to channel through the prayers of his people.

Prayer was the expression of fellowship

'When he had said this, he knelt down with all of them and prayed.' (Acts 20:36)

After three years of intensive ministry, what do we find as Paul comes to say farewell? He prays.

'We stayed with them seven days ... But when our time was up, we left and continued on our way. All the disciples and their wives and children accompanied us out of the city, and there on the beach we knelt to pray.' (Acts 21:5)

After a week's acquaintance, what do we find as Paul comes to say farewell? He prays.

It is the supreme way for Christian love to flow. It is the fastest way for brothers and sisters in Christ to go deep with one another. It is the universal language. You can pray with a group of Christians whose language you cannot understand – but no matter: you will have gone deep with them, and a bond will have been forged too deep for words. Let us never get beyond praying with one another. Some Christians have, to their loss, never begun to experience it. But it is the most natural as well as the most profound expression of fellowship between members of the same family.

There is, of course, no need to be pompous about it, or draw attention to ourselves. I think of a knot of friends in a tight circle in Durban airport, lost in prayer and only just making the flight after an insistent last call from the P.A. system! I often find myself praying with a friend over the phone, or in the street, or in a home. It is the most natural thing in the world. Of course, this naturalness can degenerate into overfamiliarity. Slouching around with our hands in our pockets is no way to address Almighty God. There is no sign of this in Paul. In both cases referred to above he is said to have knelt. Now the Bible is not fussy about posture in prayer. Standing is normal ('when you stand praying . . .'). Sitting is fine ('David sat before the Lord . . .'). And sometimes, I am glad to read, 'the saints rejoiced in their beds'! But kneeling has something that the Protestant crouch can never equal. It is an expression of deep humility before the sovereign Lord, our Maker.

Yes, prayer is indeed the supreme expression of fellowship. Let us value it and use it corporately, as Paul did on occasions like these. Praying together in the home, in small church groups, away on vacation. It is the communion of redeemed sons and daughters with their Creator who is also their Father. So both intimacy and respect are required of us. And he longs for us to come to him *together* to pray. Indeed, he offers a special promise of his nearness when believers come in twos and threes to bring their requests before him (Matthew 18:20).

Paul is indeed an example for us in prayer – not least as his friend Luke perceived him. Perhaps the most apt conclusion of this chapter might be some words of his own, repeated seven times in his letters:

'I beseech you, be followers of me.'

Through a Reader's Eyes

4

Through a Reader's Eyes

I am amazed at the constant incidental glimpses of
Paul at prayer which confront us in his letters. In
every one of his epistles we see something of this
incredible man at prayer. There are no exceptions.
Prayer is not a very prominent theme in Titus,
a brief letter to one of his lieutenants, full of
instructions on church leadership: but it is there
(Titus 1:4, 3:15). It is not prominent in Galatians,
a letter dashed off in white hot rage as he found
the church being swamped by legalism on the one
side and libertinism on the other: but it is there too
(Gal. 1:3–5; 6:16, 18).

In all of Paul's other letters prayer is either
a massive component, as in Ephesians, or else
a substantial one. I find the stress on prayer
amazing in this maverick, activist, choleric Jew
who dashed all over the known world – when he
was not languishing in prison. But for him, prayer
is a priority – whether he is writing to Timothy,

who led a chain of churches, or to Philemon, his rich landowning convert who led a house church. It makes no difference whether he is writing to an encouraging church like Philippi, or a somewhat discouraging one like Corinth; whether he is writing to people he knew well like the Philippians, or people he had never met like the Colossians. And when he is writing two general letters, both of which seem to have been intended for circulation, i.e. Romans and Ephesians, prayer comes bubbling to the surface in a big way. It is truly astonishing.

Here are five of the interesting things I have been struck by in Paul's prayer life, as flashes of it come through in the pages of his letters.

His prayers centre on the grace of God

It was grace which brought him to God in the first place: the sheer undeserved favour from the Lord himself to an arrogant, undeserving Pharisee. And Paul had an ever-deepening awareness of it. It was grace which called him, though he was not fit to be ranked an apostle (1 Cor. 15:9–11). It was grace which drove him to his knees in awe and wonder that even he could be useful to God in proclaiming the story of his mercy to those who had never heard

(Eph. 3:8). And it was the sheer grace of God which became more and more precious to him the older he got. It comes to a crescendo in one of his last letters, 1 Timothy 1:12–17.

'I thank Christ Jesus our Lord, who has given me strength, that he considered me faithful, appointing me to his service. Even though I was once a blasphemer and a persecutor and a violent man, I was shown mercy because I acted in ignorance and unbelief. The grace of our Lord was poured out on me abundantly, along with the faith and love that are in Christ Jesus.

Here is a trustworthy saying that deserves full acceptance: Christ Jesus came into the world to save sinners – of whom I am the worst. But for that very reason I was shown mercy so that in me, the worst of sinners, Christ Jesus might display his unlimited patience as an example for those who would believe on him and receive eternal life. Now to the King eternal, immortal, invisible, the only God, be honour and glory for ever and ever. Amen.'

That is the theme which dominated his life – the undeserved generosity of God. He knows himself to be utterly undeserving in God's sight, and yet the good Lord has had mercy on him and has entrusted to him a share in making known to others this undreamed-of offer of free acceptance by the God we have all wronged and slighted. The worst of sinners' – but rescued in order to be 'an example for those who would believe' across the world and down the centuries. No wonder he erupts in praise!

And it is this grace which his congregations need. So that is what, above all else, he prays for. You find it at the start of his letters, such as 1 Corinthians 1:3, 2 Corinthians 1:2, 1 Thessalonians 1:1, Galatians 1:3 and elsewhere. You find it at the end of his letters, such as Philemon verse 25, 2 Thessalonians 3:18, Galatians 6:18 and Ephesians 6:24. From first to last the Christian life is one of experiencing God's grace, and prayer is the instrument God delights to use in order to enable people to grasp it.

'Grace' has a many-sided splendour. When the believer comes to God in the first instance, it is grace, perceived as unmerited favour, which accepts him.

'It is by grace you have been saved' (Eph. 2:5).

'Grace' there manifestly means the undeserved acceptance of sinful people like us by the God who owes us nothing, but loves us just the same. And in prayer for others, there is no higher thing we could pray for than that they might come to appreciate this in their own lives.

Once they have done so, they are called to a life of progressive holiness, just as their heavenly Father is holy (1 Peter 1:15). But this is beyond the power of human beings, prone as we all are to slip and fail. And so this sheer unmerited grace of God takes on another shade of meaning: strength.

'He said to me, "My grace is sufficient for you, for my power is made perfect in weakness." Therefore I will boast all the more gladly about my weaknesses, so that Christ's power may rest on me' (2 Cor. 12:9).

That is what we need if we are to even begin to live the Christian life – the Lord's 'grace', his power to overcome the downward forces which plague us. No wonder that grace is a prominent part of the prayer of Paul for his believing friends.

But 'grace' comes to have yet a third meaning: graciousness.

'Let your conversation be always full of grace, seasoned with salt, so that you may know how to answer everyone' (Col. 4:6).

One of the manifest marks of the Lord's strength

in our lives comes precisely here, in our conversation: if we really are drawing on his strength, we shall exhibit a new graciousness in the way we talk to others. Undeserved love accepting us just as we are; undeserved strength enabling us to live for him; and undreamed of graciousness in speech as the love and power of the Lord begin to grip us and work through us. No wonder Paul prayed for grace in his converts. What higher thing could he have asked for them?

Often Paul joins 'peace' with 'grace' in his prayers for his friends. In greetings like Colossians 1:2, 1 Thessalonians 1:1, 2 Thessalonians 1:2, 1 Timothy 1:2 and so forth he longs for the peace of God to mark the lives of those in whom his grace is active.

Sometimes it is the merciful aspect of the grace of God that strikes the apostle as he prays (Gal. 6:16, 1 Tim. 1:2, 2 Tim. 1:2).

Sometimes this 'grace' is attributed simply to God (2 Cor. 1:12). Generally it is seen to come 'from God the Father and our Lord Jesus Christ' (e.g. Rom. 1:7, 1 Cor. 1:3, 2 Cor. 1:2). Sometimes Paul alludes to it in a fully trinitarian manner, as in the famous 'grace' of 2 Corinthians 13:14, 'The grace of the Lord Jesus Christ, and the love of God, and the fellowship of the Holy Spirit be with you all.'

Sometimes, as in Galatians 1:3*f.*, the mention

of the Lord's grace to us leads into some further exploration of what it means.

But always grace is central to the prayers of Paul. This is what had made a new man of him. This is his supreme desire for his churches and the individuals within them. All they need is more of the grace of God, the generous God who gives himself continuously to us in order to meet our varied needs.

His prayers are for character, not for things

If the prayers of an average modern Christian were to undergo scrutiny, we would be likely to find that prayer for specific things predominates. Prayer for health, for financial needs, for success in examinations, sport or career.

These concerns are strikingly absent from the apostle's prayers, though he was exposed to such a variety of hardships that we might have imagined that they would be prominent. His concern for his friends was not so much the meeting of particular physical and emotional needs but for growth in maturity and Christlikeness. We shall see this later when we come to look at his prayers for the Colossians (pp.79*ff*.), but it is everywhere apparent. He wants the Philippians to grow in love, discernment and the fruitfulness of a blameless Christian life (Phil. 1:9–11). Like his friend Epaphras, he prays for his readers to become mature and assured in all the will of God (Col. 4:12). To his troublesome followers in Thessalonica he writes:

'We constantly pray for you, that our God may count you worthy of his calling, and that by his power he may fulfil every good purpose of yours and every act prompted by your faith. We pray this so that the name of our Lord Jesus may be glorified in you, and you in him, according to the grace of our God and the Lord Jesus Christ' (2 Thess. 1:11–12).

If Christians learnt to do this more often, there would be less complaining at the failure by God to answer our prayers. He is not some heavenly superstore to supply our shopping lists. He is the high and holy one who inhabits eternity, and is bent on preparing his children to share it with him for ever. He wants us to 'be conformed to the likeness of his Son' (Rom. 8:29).

His prayers are informed and specific

What has just been said should not lead us to suppose that Paul engaged in banal generalities in his prayers. He did not. They were designed for the maturing of his readers and the glory of God: true enough; but they were very specific, all the same. If our prayers are vague we shall never notice any response to them.

No, there was nothing vague about his prayers. We find in his writings prayers for leaders of the nations and others in responsible positions: not only for themselves, but that, by good government, they could help to induce a climate of peace, godliness and mutual respect. Happy the country so governed! We find prayers for peace of mind in the midst of worry (Phil. 4:6). We find prayers for travel plans: Paul expects Philemon's prayers to be effective in his release (Philemon v.22). We find prayers that he be delivered from violent opponents of the gospel not so much for his own sake, but for the sake of the financial offering he was collecting from Gentile churches to give to the church at Jerusalem (Rom. 15:31). A similar prayer request for deliverance from wicked men is to be found in 2 Thessalonians 3:2, but once again it is not merely for Paul's own well being; but rather 'that the word of the Lord may spread rapidly and be honoured.'

No less specific are his prayers for interpretation if anyone uses the gift of tongues (1 Cor. 14:13). Otherwise how can a person who does not have that gift understand what is being said, and say 'Amen'?

(v.16). Not only does he pray for interpretation but also for the gift of tongues itself. It is fashionable in some circles today to overplay Paul's caution about the use of tongues in the community. To be sure he does not have any time for those who show off with the gift, for those who value unintelligibility as a mark of the divine, for those who make a display of their gift where there is no interpretation available. But he is quite clear that he wants them all to speak in tongues, though he would rather they possessed the more direct prophetic gift, so that the congregation can be built up (14:4–5). All this he makes a matter of prayer. But most of all he covets prayer for the gospel and its spread:

> 'Devote yourselves to prayer, being watchful and thankful. And pray for us, too, that God may open a door for our message, so that we may proclaim the mystery of Christ, for which I am in chains. Pray that I may proclaim it clearly, as I should' (Col. 4:2–4).

or

> '. . . always keep on praying for all the saints. Pray also for me, that whenever I open my mouth, words may be given me so that I will fearlessly make known the mystery of the gospel, for which I am an ambassador in chains' (Eph. 6:18f.).

Supremely his missionary concern is for his own nation, the Jewish people:

'Brothers, my heart's desire and prayer to God for the Israelites is that they may be saved' (Rom. 10:1).

All this is very different from many a modern churchman who is dubious about the propriety of evangelism in the first place, and of evangelising men and women of other faiths in particular. After all, we live in a pluralist society, they claim. Ah, but the Roman Empire was far more pluralist, and it was in that pluralist Roman Empire that the gospel of Christ rang out loud, clear, and distinct. Paul's prayer was that its message might be even more clear and powerful.

But not only were Paul's prayers specific. They were well informed. Even in a spiritually mixed situation like Corinth we find him thanking God for their gifts, and for the grace of God so evident among them. He was able then to write to them with knowledge and to pray for them with confidence. You can imagine him squeezing every drop of local information from the visitors from Chloe's household (1 Cor. 1:11) who brought him news. Exactly the same thing happens when Epaphroditus brings Paul news of the church in Philippi, together with a gift from them. The excitement is as unmistakable as the information with which his prayers are tinged (Phil. 4:18*f.*, 2:25–30, 1:3–11 and 15*ff.*). It is exactly the same story with the Colossians. Paul's prayers for them are stimulated when information about their turning to God arrives via Epaphras, one of their number who came to visit the apostle (Col. 1:3–9). But of that more anon (pp.97*ff.*).

Armed with that information, the apostle goes to prayer, and one of the lovely minor keys in the Epistles is the undercurrent of prayer for particular churches, which he 'mentions' in his prayers as a result: Rome (Rom. 1:9), Thessalonica (1 Thess. 1:2), Philippi (Phil. 1:3) and Ephesus (Eph. 1:16). And, astonishing to relate, we find the same informed prayer and vivid memory operating for individuals as well as churches: Philemon, for example (Philemon v.4), and Timothy (2 Tim. 1:3). I find that very encouraging. It is clearly not the length of our prayers that matters, but the intention: bringing people or congregations to mind in the presence of the Lord.

His prayers were prompted by the Spirit, not demanding of the Lord

We must never hammer at the door of heaven and seek to impose our will, as if upon a reluctant God.

There is a fine line between persistence in prayer and insistence on our own wishes. Paul's determination to subordinate his strong preferences to whatever the purpose of God may turn out to be is shown in Romans chapter 1:

> 'I remember you in my prayers at all times; and I pray that now at last by God's will the way may be opened for me to come to you . . . I do not want you to be unaware, brothers, that I planned many times to come to you (but have been prevented from doing so until now)' (Rom. 1:10, 13).

Like his Master before him, Paul's supreme desire, no matter what his personal preference, was 'Not my will, but Thine be done'. And it was when he was not pushing his own way, but allowing the Spirit to prompt prayers within him, that he was most confident of a positive answer. There is a marvellous passage in Romans 8 where he writes about this.

> 'The Spirit helps us in our weakness. We do not know what we ought to pray for, but the Spirit himself intercedes for us with groans that words cannot express. And he who searches our hearts knows the mind of the Spirit, because the Spirit intercedes for the saints in accordance with God's will' (Rom 8:26, 27).

Paul has already made it plain that one of the
surest marks of being a Christian is the presence of
the Holy Spirit in our hearts, enabling us to look up
to God and call him 'Abba, Daddy' (Rom. 8:15). He
is the member of the Godhead who resides within
the heart of the believer. And it is when he prompts
prayers within us and we turn to the Father with
them in the name of Jesus, that we can be most
confident that the Father knows what is in the mind
of the Spirit, and will answer it positively. An aston-
ishingly trinitarian understanding of prayer! And a
great encouragement to us to wait on God and allow
his Spirit, like a spring in the ground of our hearts,
to bubble up with the matters for which we should
be praying. It is like deep calling to deep when the
Father hears and interprets the groanings of the
Spirit on our behalf. Indeed, a possible translation
of Romans 8:28 is rooted in this same thought:

> 'The Spirit pleads for God's own people in God's
> own way, and in everything he cooperates for
> good with those who are called by God's purpose.'

He knows a variety of moods in prayer

At times prayer is, as we have seen, a matter of
remembering people and needs before the Lord:

simply recounting them in his presence. At times it is the gentle resting in God and his love, the profound openness to him without words or petitions: and it is in this attitude of quiet adoration that prophecy is most likely to occur.

1 Corinthians 11:4f. seems to suggest that as a man or woman adopts the appropriate attitude of awe in the gatherings of the church, God is most readily able to communicate directly with the people through an utterance which he inspires. I recall only the other day a time of waiting upon the Holy Spirit in total silence and adoration in a meeting; and not only did a glow develop on many faces, and tears wet some eyes; but somebody spoke in tongues, followed by a marvellous interpretation, and a most encouraging prophetic utterance – and it all happened to the utter amazement of one and all in a congregation where these things simply did not happen! There is no way it could have been learned behaviour or psychologically induced. It was simply the Lord breaking gently in upon his people who were turned to him in quiet expectation.

At other times prayer is marked by exultant praise and adoration, like St Paul's prayer at the outset of Ephesians 1. His prayer begins (v.3, RSV):

'Blessed be the God and Father of our Lord Jesus

Christ, who has blessed us in Christ with every spiritual blessing in the heavenly places . . .'

That too is part of prayer.

But so is deep contemplation of the living God and his abundant love. That is what we find in the very same letter, Ephesians 3:14*ff.* We shall be looking at it more closely later, but it is a profoundly moving picture of Paul the man of prayer on his knees before his heavenly Father, simply weighed down with amazement at the length and breadth and depth and height of the love of this God who has deigned to allow Christ to come and dwell in his heart in response to his cry of faith. It is in such contemplation that the human spirit is taken beyond itself and deeply nourished.

At times Paul breaks his sequence of thought simply in order to burst out in praise. 2 Corinthians 2:14 is a good example, as is Romans 9:5 or 1 Timothy 1:17. I love that instinctive apostrophe, that lifting of the eyes to the Lord to say 'You are wonderful'. Many of the deepest moments in my own prayer life are prompted by occasions when I do just that – drop everything and simply turn to him in short but heartfelt praise. It is one of the ways of what Brother Lawrence would call practising the presence of Christ.

At times, prayer is the means whereby the believer receives visions: it clearly was for Paul

(2 Cor. 10:3*f*.). At times prayer is particularly directed towards evangelism (Rom. 1:9). Paul and his friends knew times when there was an acute battle in prayer (Eph. 6:18*ff*.), or 'agonising' prayer as he calls it in Colossians (4:12). That is the language of intensely active wrestling. It is the word used of Jesus' prayer in the Garden (Luke 22:44). Paul knew that there is a great outside hindrance to our prayers, Satan. He knew that human effort alone counted for little, but that prayer did.

> 'For though we live in the world, we do not wage war as the world does. The weapons we fight with are not the weapons of the world. On the contrary, they have divine power to demolish strongholds' (2 Cor. 10:3–4).

The modern church in the West knows little of prayer against the forces of darkness like this, but there are signs that as the fascination of the occult and overt Satanism increase some Christians are beginning to awake to the importance of spiritual warfare through prayer and fasting. At all events, there is no doubt that it figured rather significantly in Paul's many-sided understanding of prayer. It is therefore with no exaggeration that he can advise his friends in Thessalonica, 'Pray without ceasing' (1 Thess. 5:17). This is what he had himself learned to do. Prayer without leaving long gaps (*adialeiptōs*) is one of the great secrets of successful Christian living. Indeed, no Christian living can be fruitful without it.

For Missions

5

For Missions

Most of us find prayer for missionary work very
difficult. It is so hard to project ourselves into a
foreign country, with different language, different
customs, different lifestyles. How shall we pray
for such people? How shall we pray for friends,
perhaps, who have left these shores to go and
spread the gospel among them? I know I find it
difficult – and I have a son working his heart out to
make Christ known half a world away in a Muslim
land. I would find it a lot more difficult if I did not
have that strong personal link. It is not surprising,
then, if, in our prayers for Christians we have never
seen, in a land we do not know, we resort to a vague,
blanket prayer, 'Lord, bless them anyway'.

It was not like that with the apostle Paul.

He is writing from prison. He has a small group of
Christian friends around him, who apparently are
free to go where they please. And he sends two of
them to a church he has never seen, the Christian

community at a place called Colossae. We do not
know for sure where Paul was imprisoned when he
wrote this letter: probably Rome. We do not know
when Colossae began to respond to the gospel of
Christ: probably in the mid-fifties of the first cen-
tury when Paul was at the height of his influence
at Ephesus, speaking boldly and persuasively about
the good news of Jesus in the School of Tyrannus on
a daily basis. We are told that 'this continued for
two years, so that all the residents of Asia heard
the word of the Lord, both Jews and Greeks' (Acts
19:9*f*.). Colossae was a town situated in the Lycus
Valley, on the main road from Ephesus to the East.
One of Paul's Christian friends, Epaphras, clearly
played a leading part in church planting here, and
it was he who brought to the apostle the news about
the Colossian church which sparked the Epistle to
the Colossians which we have in our Bible. Paul
makes it plain that he had never met them (Col. 2:1)
though he longed to do so. So his prayer for them is
a prime example of the way he prayed for missions
and interceded powerfully and imaginatively for
fellow believers who were utter strangers to him.
It may well be that we have a good deal to learn
from his example.

The apostle's prayer

'And so, from the day we heard of it, we have
not ceased to pray for you, asking that you may
be filled with the knowledge of his will in all
spiritual wisdom and understanding, to lead a
life worthy of the Lord, fully pleasing to him,
bearing fruit in every good work and increasing
in the knowledge of God. May you be strengthened with all power, according to his glorious
might, for all endurance and patience with joy,
giving thanks to the Father, who has qualified
us to share in the inheritance of the saints in
light. He has delivered us from the dominion of
darkness and transferred us to the kingdom of
his beloved Son, in whom we have redemption,
the forgiveness of sins' (Col. 1:9–14, RSV).

The characteristics of his prayer

A number of things stand out as we read a prayer
like this, and try to put ourselves in his shoes as he
lies there in prison.

His prayer was *immediate*. As soon as he heard
the news from Epaphras, he prayed. Here is a man
who turns news items into prayer. He does not
wait until his evening devotions. He prays then

and there. That has influenced me a great deal. Nowadays when someone asks me to pray about a matter, and I agree, I stop then and there and commit it to the Lord – even if we happen to be standing in the street.

His prayer was *informed*. You can imagine him chatting enthusiastically with Epaphras, anxious to glean all the information he could about this exciting new church which nevertheless betrayed dangerous tendencies. If our prayers are to be effective, especially for those we do not know, it is important to get informed. And this is where slides, videos, missionary magazines and personal friendships with those who know the place for which we are praying are invaluable.

His prayer was *persistent*, 'from the day we heard of it'. On and on he prayed. He did not pray once and then forget all about it. He steadily set himself to intercede (and only then did he take up pen to write to them). God has his own reasons for delaying a reply to our prayers. Sometimes it is to test our sincerity, and see if we really desire what we have prayed for.

His prayer was *loving*. At least, 'praying and asking' suggests that to me. He meant business, because he cared about them. 'I want you to know how greatly I strive for you ... and for all who have not seen my face, that their hearts may be encouraged as they are knit together in love' (Col.

2:1*f*., RSV). True prayer is the overflow of love towards both God and man.

His prayer was *corporate*, 'from the day we heard of it'. He had clearly gathered Epaphras and Onesimus, Tychicus and Aristarchus together for prayer about the situation at Colossae. I would love to have been a fly on the wall at those prayer meetings. The unity of spirit, the participation by one and all, the earnestness, the love, the sanctified imagination in their prayers would have taught me so much. Prayer does not need to be either solitary or confined to liturgical settings, valid though both are. These prayers were held corporately, informally, and no doubt very uncomfortably on the floor of a Roman prison!

His prayer was *grateful*. A few verses earlier, at the very start of the letter, Paul exclaims 'We always thank God, the Father of our Lord Jesus Christ, when we pray for you, because we have heard of your faith ... and love ... and hope'. He thanks God, too, for the way the gospel bears fruit and grows among them as it does throughout the world. He will have some tough things to say to them later on. But he begins with heartfelt gratitude that they have entrusted their lives to Christ and are beginning to manifest his love and faith and hope and impact. Here again, he is an example to us.

His prayer was *costly*. When he speaks in chapter

2:1 about 'how greatly I strive for you' he uses a very powerful word, *agōn* meaning literally a battle, a contest, a wrestling match. It is, as we have seen, the word used of Jesus praying with intense passion in the Garden of Gethsemane. It is the same word used of Epaphras, who wrestles for his dear friends at Colossae as he prays for them (Col. 4:12). Prayer is hard work. It is not hard only because we are lazy, and weak, and forgetful, and earthbound. It is hard because there is a great external hindrance to prayer. Satan is a reality. There is a war on. Prayer keeps the communication lines open with God, the only source of our strength. And for that very reason, it will be relentlessly attacked by the enemy of souls. If he can isolate us from God, he has us at his mercy. Our prayers will be rendered ineffective and our lives will fall an easy prey to his assaults. Twentieth-century Christians need to wake up to the vital importance of costly, determined prayer which confronts the principalities and powers of darkness (*cf.* Eph. 6:10–20) and loosens their unseen grip on circumstances and people. Alien though all this is to our sceptical, secularised minds, prayer involves spiritual battle. And those who are most willing to enter into the battle are those who most frequently see their prayers answered.

His prayer was *unselfish*. He did not 'dump' his own problems on the Colossians, great though these were. He was lonely, cold, hungry, imprisoned, and unable to pursue his vocation. But not a word of all this as he writes to them. He is entirely concerned for them, their welfare and their growth. If we pay too much attention to our own concerns we will never grow in maturity and sympathy: we will come to think that the world should centre upon ourselves, and we will shrivel in consequence.

The contents of his prayer

I find it absolutely fascinating to overhear the apostle at prayer for this church of strangers. Not 'God bless the Colossians' or 'We remember before you the church at Colossae', but powerful, intentional, specific intercession. And if you think that it is not possible to pray specifically for those whose situation you do not really understand, then read on! This is how Paul did it. In short, he prayed for knowledge, for obedience, and for strength.

He prayed that they should know God's will

Nothing could be more important for the Christian than knowing God's will. It was the keynote of Jesus' own life: 'I always do what pleases him', he said, of his relation with his heavenly Father (John 8:29). And as he faced the appalling destiny of the cross, and naturally shrank from it, he prayed, 'yet not my will, but yours be done' (Luke 22:42). He taught his disciples to pray 'your will be done on earth as it is in heaven' (Matt. 6:10). That should be the goal of our lives.

And yet it is so difficult. We wish we knew what God's will was on this or that matter. We wish we could read it off like the text on the screen of a computer when we press the appropriate keys. We all know that it is not like that. But the question of God's will is not all that obscure, either. A great deal of his will is made known to us in the Bible: more than enough to live by.

It is as we and those we pray for study it on a regular basis that we will have a growing awareness of God's will. It makes sense to pray that those who have come to faith may realise the purposes for which God has called them, and be able to discern his will for their lives. There must be no place for obscurantism in the Christian life: knowledge is not to be eschewed, but welcomed, so long as it issues not in pride but in obedience. Indeed full knowledge is the greatest safeguard against error. And Christian wisdom (*sophia*) and Christian shrewdness of perception (*sunesis*) are two of the choicest blessings God can bestow. This overall understanding of his will, this occasional flash of insight into his purposes, generally comes through patient daily study of the Word of God, and a willingness to follow it. That is the sort of person to whom God can disclose his will. And one of the most important things we can do for others, whether we have met them or not, is to pray, like Paul, that they 'may be filled with the knowledge of his will in all wisdom and spiritual understanding'.

He prayed that they should fulfil God's will

Knowledge is never an end in itself. It is meant to lead to obedience. God does not reveal to us many things we would love to know: he shows us enough light to walk by. He does not commit himself to answering our speculative questions, like 'Why should suffering occur?' or 'What becomes of those who have not heard the gospel?' No, he expects his truth to be obeyed, not trifled with. It is his responsibility to reveal his will to us. It is ours to obey it. And that is the second thing that Paul prays for the Colossians. He wants them to know God's purpose for their lives, and he wants them to achieve it. He sums up in a succinct sentence the life of the person who obeys God's will.

It will be a *consistent* life ('a life worthy of the Lord'). A life that is a credit to Jesus Christ. If church people lived like that, there would be an infinitely greater hunger in society to know the reason why! What a way to pray for others: that they may lead lives that are worthy of Jesus.

It will be a *sensitive* life ('fully pleasing to him'). Here is a marvellous touchstone of authentic Christian ethics. They do not consist of slavish obedience to some rule book, but of loving devotion to a person. I find it significant that the New Testament is very short on specific ethical injunctions: but this idea of seeking to please Jesus in everything we do is central. It is wonderfully flexible: it allows full room for variety in our personalities and perceptions of Jesus. It is wonderfully liberating: not legislation but love relationship. It is so wonderfully creative, too: if we really seek to please him in all we do, all manner of new initiatives will emerge. We shall not be bound by the past, but shall be free to, as Augustine put it, 'love God – and do what you like'. The world needs liberated Christians like that. We do well to pray for them.

It will be a *fruitful* life ('bearing fruit in every good work'). 'Fruitful' is an evocative word. It conjures up images of trees laden with fruit, fulfilling the purpose of their existence. I want Christians to be like that! So I need to pray it into being for those for whom I intercede. 'Fruit' in the New Testament is primarily used to describe the qualities of character which will emerge as we keep in close touch with Christ. 'Love, joy, peace, patience, kindness, goodness, faithfulness, gentleness, self-control' – these

are the 'fruit' or 'crop' produced by the Spirit of
Jesus indwelling us (Gal. 5:22). Equally, when we
help others to come to Christ, that too is 'fruit' or
'harvest'. And so Paul prays that he may come to
Rome to 'reap a harvest' among them 'as among
other Gentiles' (Rom. 1:13). But neither the fruit
of character nor of evangelism will be found in us
unless we abide in Christ the Vine (John 15:1–17).
Without him we can bear no fruit. Cut off from him
we are just dead branches. That is what Paul is
getting at as he prays for fruitful Christian lives
at Colossae.

It will also be a *deepening* life ('increasing in the
knowledge of God'). How sad it is to see Christians
who have 'died' two or three decades ago. The same
old ideas, the same old expressions, the same old
prejudices as long ago. It is all too possible to
get stuck spiritually. The water of life in which
Christians were spawned somehow gets frozen –
and they with it! This is very sad. It is precisely
the opposite of what God wants. He longs for us to
grow in our knowledge of him – not just of his will.
In Islam, Allah reveals his will to mortal man: never
his person. But that is just what the God revealed
to us in Scripture delights to do. He wants us to
know him, in increasing depth and intimacy, as
the years go by. How important, then, to pray that
this may be true in the lives of those for whom we
intercede.

He prayed that they should be empowered to fulfil God's will

Knowledge, obedience, strength. What a trio of spiritual qualities! Paul is well aware that the Lord enables what he commands. He does not ask the impossible of us. No, for 'where the word of a king is, there is power' (Eccles. 8:4, AV). One of the most amazing things about God is that he sets us the highest standards, and then offers us the power to at least begin to achieve those standards, slow though the progress is! It encourages me not a little to read that the Lord supplies me with the power to obey the requirements that he asks of me.

Notice, first, the *extent* of this power. It is limitless. It is 'in line with the power of his glory'. Not some second rate enabling, but God's glory at work in equipping weak sinners to share that glory. 'Glory' is a deep word in the Bible. In the Old Testament it has the nuance of weight and solidity: in the New Testament it carries the overtones of splendour and light. Both, of course, are essentially attributes of God himself. And he has the power to begin the transformation of even such intractable material as ourselves in the direction of glory.

Second, notice the *effect* of this power. It was Lord Acton who once observed: 'All power tends to corrupt: absolute power tends to corrupt absolutely.' How true! But not God's power. The result of his empowering is stated very clearly. It results in 'all endurance and patience with joy'. When God's power is welcomed into our hearts it does not make us big headed but humble hearted. It produces not arrogance, but patient endurance with joy. The endurance of prisoners languishing in gaol for the sake of Christ. The patience of missionaries working for decades in situations where they see no fruit. The joy of people like Mother Theresa who, humanly speaking, have so little to be joyful about. These are the marks, these are the manifestations of the power God wants to instil into his children. Such power changes lives.

You will have noticed that these three great requests, for knowledge, obedience and strength, are all highly specific, but they are applicable to Christians everywhere, not least to those for whom we are asked to pray but have never met. There is nothing vague about them: they are precise and measurable. They are rooted in God's self-revelation in the Scriptures. And they are bathed in love, the love with which Paul himself was daily washed by the heavenly Father. We need prayer like that to ricochet around the world.

The conclusion of his prayer

Paul ends his prayer, just as he began his reflections on these Colossian Christians, with thanksgiving. Clearly it came naturally to him. Thanksgiving before he prays. Thanksgiving afterwards (Col. 1:12–14). It is a lovely trait to cultivate. It comes bursting out in Paul in many places (e.g. Rom. 9:5, 2 Tim. 1:17). It is very notable in Peter's first letter where it erupts like a volcano at the very outset, as he recalls the resurrection of Jesus which transformed his own life (1 Peter 1:3). Some years ago there was a 'praise' movement which set about praising God for whatever happened: there is a lot to be said for it. More recently, thousands of people have been marching in the streets of many countries to praise God and celebrate his power and goodness: there's a lot to be said for that, too. Praise and thanksgiving have many effects. They keep us grateful and remind us of God's greatness and of our own smallness. They keep us on the lookout for answers to our prayers. Thanksgiving as we pray for others enables us to keep mental track of the growth they have been making, and encourages us to further petition. And as God is praised and celebrated in the streets it brings an intangible but real sense of his presence and victory in the locality. Paul, at all events, made praise so much a priority that it became second nature to him.

There are two things in particular for which Paul gives thanks here.

First, he thanks God for their *new status*. The

Father has qualified them to share in the inheritance of the saints in light. 'Saints' is their description: it is applied in the New Testament to all Christians, people who are, literally, 'set aside' for him. 'Light' is their address, so to speak. They used to inhabit the country of darkness. Now that they have come to Christ, they have discovered a totally undreamed-of inheritance. They live in God's country, the Land of Light. The contrast is as striking as that. They have a totally new spiritual address: a new status; a new citizenship. This is something they can be sure about, and without a suspicion of arrogance or smugness. For it is God (and not themselves) who has qualified them.

Second, Paul thanks God for their *mighty Saviour*. Sometimes great theologians lose sight of the basics, and find the forms of expression they used years ago to be open to misunderstanding. So they tend to become more opaque, more cautious. Not so St Paul, one of the greatest theologians who ever lived. He is very robust and very decisive in describing the change which their conversion has brought about. Words like liberation, transfer, rescue and pardon jostle one another from his pen. Instead of bondage – release. Instead of darkness – light. Instead of alienation from God – the inheritance with the saints. Instead of unbearable guilt – the forgiveness of sins!

What a prayer! What a thanksgiving! And all for

people he had never met, as he lay in his prison thinking about them and praying for them. What a stimulus to our prayers for missions.

For a Church He Knew Well

6

For a Church He Knew Well

Philippi! How the Apostle Paul thrilled to that
name. It meant a great deal in the course of his
ministry. For it had been to Philippi that he had
gone when he received that vision of the man
of Macedonia beckoning him over into Europe.
Philippi was one of the foremost cities in the
great Roman province of Macedonia, comprising
the whole of Northern Greece. It was a tough nut
to crack: full of retired soldiers from the legions,
founded as a Roman colony. But it was here that
Paul managed to plant a tiny church, inaugu-
rated at the Jewish meeting place for prayer by
the river.

We know of three of its first members. One
was Lydia, a leading businesswoman. One was
a slave girl who had been deeply into the occult
and had been set free through Paul's ministry. The
third was the gaoler of the prison into which Paul
had been thrown for preaching the gospel in the

streets of the city! Hardly a promising beginning but the church grew and prospered, possibly under the guidance and pastoral care of Luke. A few years later, when the letter to the Philippians was written, it had clearly become a force to be reckoned with, complete with its own bishops and deacons (Phil. 1:1) and its own dynamic and generous, if occasionally disruptive, church life.

So it is no surprise that Paul is full of warmth as he set about writing to this church that he had evangelised some ten years earlier. Not for the first time he was in prison, and it appears that they had just sent him a gift of money, and probably provisions, through one of their number, a man called Epaphroditus (2:25*ff*.). He writes to thank them and to deal with a number of other issues. But first and foremost we find him at prayer for them.

The apostle's prayer

'I thank my God in all my remembrance of you, always in every prayer of mine for you all making my prayer with joy, thankful for your partnership in the gospel from the first day until now. And I am sure that he who began a good work in you will bring it to completion at the day of Jesus Christ.

It is right for me to feel thus about you all, because I hold you in my heart, for you are all partakers with me of grace, both in my imprisonment and in the defence and confirmation of the gospel. For God is my witness, how I yearn for you all with the affection of Christ Jesus.

And it is my prayer that your love may abound more and more, with knowledge and all discernment, so that you may approve what is excellent, and may be pure and blameless for the day of Christ, filled with the fruits of righteousness which come through Jesus Christ, to the glory and praise of God' (Phil. 1:3–11, RSV).

Paul's approach to prayer

Not surprisingly, Paul's approach is not very different from the way in which he prayed for the Colossians. Once we have formed good habits in prayer, they tend to serve us well.

His prayer was *regular* – 'in all my remembrance of you'. I do not suppose that he spent a great deal of time in prayer each time he remembered them but recall them he did, and he turned recollection into prayer. I am struck by the number of times that phrases like 'making mention of you in my prayers' come in the New Testament. They point to Christians who were living so close to God that memory flowed naturally into prayer: and those prayers may have been frequent rather than extended.

His prayer was *thankful* – 'I thank my God'. I would love it if gratitude could be picked out as one of the major strands in my prayer life. I fear that all too often I am insistent in asking and forgetful to come back and thank God for what he has done. Paul did not make that mistake. Thankfulness marks his prayers. It is, in fact, a hallmark of authentic spirituality.

His prayer was *joyful* – 'making my prayer with joy'. Often prayer seems a drudgery, a duty, but no joy. Often in corporate prayer, requests seem to be a solemn rigmarole rather than joyful interaction with a generous God. Joy was one of the most notable characteristics of Jesus: this is what drew so many different types of people to him. He was so radiantly alive. And he promised that his joy would remain as a gift to his followers (John 15:11). Alas, it is a gift that many have never unpacked.

His prayer was *reflective* – 'my remembrance of you'. As he prayed, he must, on occasions, have given himself time to reflect over them, and recall all that had taken place 'from the first day until now'. What memories must have flooded into his mind! The eight-mile tramp down the Via Egnatia from the port of Neapolis to the open air prayer place. Lydia 'whose heart the Lord opened' ('Lord',

he might have mused, 'please keep Lydia's heart
open to you'). The gaoler ('Lord, keep him safe with
you'), the slave girl ('Lord, do not allow those evil
forces to come back and dominate her life. Protect
her, Lord Jesus'). The magistrates who had thrown
him and Silas into prison ('Lord, get through to
them in your own time and your own way'). As
he reflected on people and events there, it is little
wonder that memory led into thanksgiving for the
church at Philippi, their conversion, their growth,
their care for him, their zeal in evangelism. And in
turn, thanksgiving made way for intercession.

Paul's grounds for prayer

Why did Paul bother to give so much time and care
to intercession for his friends and their churches?
It is, after all, very hard work, if you are going
to sustain it week after week, year after year.
Why bother? He gives us three reasons that may
encourage us to bother.

Because of his affinity with them
(Phil. 1:5)
Twice in rapid succession Paul uses the key Christian word for fellowship, *koinonia*. It lurks under
the English words translated 'partnership' and
'partakers'. It means joint participation, sharing
in something together. What, you may ask, did

this mercurial apostle share in common with the retired sergeant majors at Philippi? He mentions three things in particular.

They shared a common gospel (verse 5). It was the same good news of Jesus the Saviour and Lord which had brought this proud Pharisee to his knees and had penetrated to the Roman colony in Philippi. The gospel had made new people of both Paul and the Philippians. And this is a powerful inducement to prayer, especially prayer for those we have led to faith. This same mighty instrument of God's good news operates everywhere, and because we share it together we can pray with great joy and confidence for one another. Pray for your converts. You share a common gospel.

What is more, they shared a common task (verse 7). It was the 'defence and confirmation of the gospel'. Peter uses this same Greek word, 'defence', when he encourages his readers 'Always be prepared to make a defence to any one who calls you to account for the hope that is in you, yet do it with gentleness' (1 Peter 3:15, RSV). There are good reasons for the Christian faith: it is not the craven surrender of the intellect. And we believers need to know what we believe and why we believe. We need also to be prepared to say so, confidently and yet modestly, as opportunity offers. The other word Paul uses, 'confirmation', suggests making something firm and strong. It speaks of competent nurture of young Christians. It speaks of training Christian workers. Paul and his converts at Philippi were all involved together in this ministry of Christian apologetics and Christian nurture. It is a powerful platform on which to build reciprocal prayer, for both parties know the joys and the difficulties of what they are committed to.

Paul also reminds them that they share a common grace (verse 7). That is such an inducement to prayer, too. 'Grace', as we have seen, has at least three meanings in the New Testament writings, and here it is obvious that 'strength' is our nearest equivalent. We, and those for whom we pray, are all equally the recipients of the Lord's gracious strength for our daily battles if we ask him. The same Lord who sustains us will sustain them as we pray for them. And that is a good ground for prayer, if ever there was one.

Sharing helps praying.

Because of his assurance about God's will (Phil. 1:6)

Their perseverance these ten years had proved the reality of God's work in the Philippians. His love would not let them go. He who had begun so good a work in them would bring it to completion. Their survival and growth was guaranteed by the nature of God himself, the utterly consistent one. Paul may have been brooding recently on Psalm 138 with its wonderful words 'Though I walk in the midst of trouble, you preserve my life; you stretch out your hand against the anger of my foes, with your right hand you save me. *The LORD will fulfil his purpose for me*; your love, O LORD, endures for ever – do not abandon the works of your hands.' Yes, he who has begun ... will complete. What a picture that conjures up of the one who is both Alpha and Omega. He holds in his mighty hands both the prisoner at Rome and the congregation at Philippi. He will complete the tapestry of their lives which he has begun to weave. There is no doubt whatever about his will and his power in this matter, and so Paul prays with deep assurance.

Knowing God's will helps praying.

Because of his affectionate heart
(Phil. 1:7, 8)
'I hold you in my heart ... I yearn for you all with the affection of Jesus Christ.' There seems to be a mixture of natural affection for these bluff northerners, fractious and quarrelsome though they were; and of the *agape* love derived from the heart of Jesus himself. Natural affection is often a guide to who we should be praying for. Supernatural love is the fire which keeps it burning. Today we prize love, and despise prayer. In those days if you loved, you prayed. In Paul we see a man who lived so close to Jesus Christ that he loved with Christ's

98

affection as well as with his own natural bonds of friendship.

Loving helps praying.

Paul's requests in prayer

There is no great spread of prayers here: Paul majors on two great themes, love and fruitfulness, and he develops each as he meditates and asks.

Love

He prays for love – 'it is my prayer that your love may abound more and more.' It is the number one priority. Not sentiment, not liking, not desire, but true love. Love, *agape*, means the outgoing of the whole personality in sacrificial service. God's love is like that. He did not feel sentimental about the world, did not like it, did not have any stirrings of lust about it: no, he loved it. And that is why he sent his beloved Son to come and die and rise for us so that we could be set free to respond to such undreamed-of generosity. No wonder the early Christians practically invented the word *agape*, to denote such love. There was nothing like it in the whole wide world. *Agape* means the joining of our heart to the object of our love, and the devotion of our life to his or her good. God is like that, in his love. Jesus loved like that. And it is the supreme mark of the Master in the disciple. It is the clinching evidence that our Christian profession is real. That is why Paul prays for love in the Philippian church. It is the benchmark of belonging.

He prays for abundant love – 'abound more and more'. Paul thinks perhaps of a great river breaking its banks and flooding the meadows alongside. He longs to see in them a Christian love which reaches out, not to some, but to all; not occasionally, but habitually, not in talk, but in action. We do not manage to produce love like this. It needs constant replenishing from the spring in the heart of God himself.

He prays for increasing love – 'more and more'. Progress is an essential in all life. It certainly is in Christian discipleship. You cannot stay stationary as a Christian, any more than you can stay stationary on a bicycle. Love is the language of the Godhead. You and I can't have too much of it. Our progress in the Christian life is marked by progress in love, above all else. Nor is such love an emotional thing. It has a cognitive aspect and a practical outworking, as he makes plain in the unfolding of his prayer.

He prays for a love which deepens knowledge. Love and knowledge are not foes, but friends, and Paul knows this. So he prays first and foremost for a deeper knowledge in his Philippian congregation, a deeper knowledge of Christ. The word used for 'knowledge', *epignosis*, is usually given personal overtones in the New Testament. It does not mean knowledge in general or academic competence: it means knowledge of Jesus. Churches and theological seminaries can all too easily breed knowledge about Jesus without helping members to know him in a deeper way personally. It is that knowledge *of* Jesus that Paul is so keen to inculcate.

The love which has been deepened by growing knowledge of Jesus will speedily develop discernment. If we have learned to love Jesus we shall get better at discerning him under the cloak of daily events. Think of hunting dogs following the scent, and you will get a glowing image of what enthusiasm should mark our desire to sniff out our Lord's pleasure.

If we do that, we shall find a growing discrimination in our lives out of respect for Jesus. The Greek here is ambiguous. It could mean 'that you may discriminate between things that differ': I need that discrimination in this confusing world with its million distractions. And it could mean 'that you may approve things that are excellent'. Genuine discrimination leads the believer to make sound decisions, always seeking the best, like the Swiss mountain guide, killed in the Alps, whose tombstone read simply 'died climbing'.

And there is a deep inner logic to this prayer of Paul's. For if a love which produces discriminating knowledge is growing in us, we shall indeed be ready to meet the Lord at the 'day of Christ'. He refers, of course, to the End. For us that end may be when we die: it may be that we shall be part of that generation which is around when Jesus returns to wind up all human history. In either case it will be decisive. And if we have learned to discern him and please him under the incognito of ordinary events and ordinary challenges from ordinary people in life, we shall the more readily recognise him at the End. None of us can escape that encounter. For we are called lovingly to work out in daily behaviour the righteousness he so generously invests us with when we begin to follow him.

He prays for a love which makes a difference in daily life. Two aspects of their behaviour particularly concern him.

First, their *motives*. He wants them to be 'pure'. The word used, *eilikrinēs*, means 'sincere', or 'judged in the light of the sun'. Both translations take us back to beekeeping. Honey needed to be 'sincere' (Latin 'without wax'), and that was judged by holding the honey up to the light of the sun to see if there were particles of wax in the product. A beautiful image! Paul longs for their motives to be as pure as refined honey. And that happens when, in any doubtful matter, we give the Lord the benefit of the doubt.

Second, their *actions*. He longed for them to be *aproskopoi*, 'not stumbling blocks'. Our lives are meant to be stepping stones to Christ, not stumbling blocks. If that word 'not stumbling blocks' is taken in an active sense, it means 'giving no offence'. If you see it as passive it means 'taking no offence'. They fit together. We shall not be able to face Christ with equanimity on that Day, if our actions have caused God's little ones to stumble. 'For we must all appear before the judgment seat of Christ, so that each one may receive good or evil, according to what he has done in the body' (2 Cor. 5:10, RSV). We, too, face judgment.

Fruitfulness

If love in all its depth is one great concern of the apostle for his converts, fruitfulness is the other. We saw it when he told the Colossians about his prayers for them (Col. 1:10). An unfruitful Christian life is an insult to God and unattractive to men and women. God is like a gardener who comes seeking fruit. And when he finds lives like the barren fig tree in the Gospels, they call down his righteous judgment, his curse.

Paul longed to see a twofold fruit in the Philippians. The fruit of a holy life, pure motives, practical goodness. That was one variety. The other was the fruit of outreach with the good news – 'the defence and confirmation of the gospel'. It is clear that they were trying to do this at Philippi (Phil. 1:15*ff*.) even though some did it to spite Paul in his imprisonment, others with sincere motivation. Still they did it. There was some sort of preaching of the gospel. And for that Paul rejoiced and would continue to do so. There was no narrow party spirit about this big man. He was not looking for clones of himself, but for disciples of Jesus. Yes, they were doing this outreach, after a fashion, at Philippi. And he was doing it in prison (Phil. 1:12, 13).

His fearless explanation to his guards about why he was in prison and who Jesus was had enabled the good news to spread throughout the praetorian guard (the crack troops of the Empire, one of whose duties was to guard significant prisoners). Bars and shackles could not keep this man from spreading the gospel. It was his lifeblood. And we can be sure it was often effective. Laconically, at the end of this letter, he sends greetings from 'the saints who are of Caesar's household' (Phil. 4:22). How fruitful the gospel had proved to be in his hands if it had produced saints in Caesar's household! Of course, the ancient 'household' included all the slaves and freedmen, and, in the case of the Emperor, the praetorian guard as well.

Outreach is the lifeblood of Christianity. It is nothing to do with personality, churchmanship or denomination. God expects this twofold fruit, of holy living and outward looking, from all of us. And, praise be, he enables us to find it 'through Jesus Christ'. But how easily we lose heart! So pray for others on this score, as Paul did from his prison cell. And get others to pray for you in this matter, as Paul did when he wrote to Christians at Ephesus:

'And pray for me, that utterance may be given me in opening my mouth boldly to proclaim the mystery of the gospel, for which I am an ambassador in chains; that I may declare it boldly, as I ought to speak' (Eph. 6:19*f*., RSV).

Love that grows in knowledge and Christlikeness. Love that shows itself in fruitfulness. What more important things could you possibly ask God to do in the life of an individual or a congregation?

Paul's goal in prayer

The concluding words of this great prayer are important. Paul cherishes no illusion of empire building at Philippi for his own sake. Nor is he praying solely for the sake of his friends there. What he most longs for is God's glory!

He wants the glory of God to shine out like a beacon, so that all can see it and be attracted by it. And there, in this Roman colony, full of battle hardened old warriors, men will see God's glory as Paul himself has, and adore him for all that he is. Paul is looking, in the long run, for nothing less than a creation back in touch with its Creator, a world where God's will shall be done on earth as it is in heaven. That is how the Master taught us to pray. Should not the disciple make it his supreme goal to cooperate in a small way through his prayers with the Creator's grand, cosmic design?

For Individuals

7

For Individuals

If we were to analyse our own prayers, we would probably find that most of them are concerned with individuals. With the apostle Paul, the opposite seems to have been the case. He was more taken up with whole churches and their direction, than with the individuals within them. He cared about individuals: of course he did. The last chapter of Romans, for example, is little more than a list of such people whom he knew in the capital, without ever having been there, and for whom he must inevitably have interceded time and again. But the fact remains that in his surviving letters we do not have many examples of his prayer for individuals. However, we have some, and they are eloquent. Here are four.

A loved one

First, we see Paul at prayer for someone he loved

very deeply, Timothy. He had led Timothy to faith. He had worked with him on many evangelistic forays. He had been in prison with him. And now, himself in prison once more, Paul writes to this trusted and much loved lieutenant to encourage him in his role of leadership. 2 Timothy is the last and most intimate of Paul's letters, and it begins with prayer.

There is an interesting and suggestive sequence here.

'Paul, . . . to Timothy, my beloved child: Grace, mercy, and peace from God the Father and Christ Jesus our Lord. I thank God, whom I serve with a clear conscience, as did my fathers, when I remember you constantly in my prayers. As I remember your tears, I long night and day to see you, that I may be filled with joy. I am reminded of your sincere faith, a faith that dwelt first in your grandmother Lois and your mother Eunice, and now, I am sure, dwells in you. Hence I remind you to rekindle the gift of God that is within you . . .' (2 Tim. 1:1–6, RSV)

Ancient letters were so much more direct than ours: the normal convention was to write 'A to B, greeting' (if you were a Greek) or 'A to B, peace be with you' (if you were a Hebrew). But Paul is not bound by convention! He combines the Greek 'grace' with the Hebrew 'peace' and throws in, for good measure, 'mercy'. God does offer us his grace for all our daily needs: he does offer us his deep, enfolding peace. But above all we stand only because of his mercy to sinners like us. And Paul never forgot it, either for himself or for experienced Christians like Timothy. We never arrive at the place where we no longer need mercy.

His longing for Timothy is grace, mercy and peace, a comprehensive trio. But that petition is tinged, as ever in Paul, with gratitude and memory. He is so thankful for his beloved Timothy. And as he prays the years roll back, and he recalls Timothy's homelife – the Jewish maternal side to the family and the pagan paternal side (Acts 16:1*ff*.). He is so grateful for the heritage of faith (Jewish faith, by the way!) that enlivened at least one half of the family, grateful for the tears (were they indicative of the struggle between the believer and the pagan in Timothy's own teenage heart?), grateful for the faith that had come to mark him, grateful for the gift of God which indwelt Timothy, the Holy Spirit himself. Paul had a lot to give thanks for, and he allows imagination and memory to prompt him into praise and thanksgiving. We have noted that thankful streak already in Paul's prayer life; just as we have taken note of his emphasis on memory and the part which that plays in intercession. Nowhere is it more strongly stressed than here: 'I remember you constantly in my prayers ... I remember ... I am reminded ... I remind you.' Mental imagery is suspect in some Christian circles, but it is an important element in the life of prayer. It is such a help to recall a mental picture of the one for whom we pray, and allow that to direct us into sensitive intercession. And don't you find the 'night and day' allusion poignant? Paul is imprisoned in very tough circumstances, possibly in the Mamertime Prison in Rome – a real hell hole – and 'night and day' probably reflect the pain, the sleeplessness and the cold to which he was exposed. How easy it would have been to give way to fruitless frustration. Instead he turned those wakeful hours into the fruitful channel of prayer. And many a Christian invalid has taken the same, courageous path. Personally, I find I do a good deal of praying in bed when I cannot get to sleep. I ask the Lord what he wants to teach me by the sleeplessness, and then whom he wants me to pray for.

Quite a sequence, is it not? *Remembering*, *thanking*, *praying*, and only then *reminding* Timothy of things he needs to keep in mind. It is a pattern we could well adopt.

A benefactor

We find a second personal prayer of Paul's in a tantalising section of the same chapter.

'May the Lord grant mercy to the household of Onesiphorus, for he often refreshed me; he was not ashamed of my chains, but when he arrived in Rome he searched for me eagerly and found me – may the Lord grant him to find mercy from the Lord on that Day – and you well know the service he rendered at Ephesus.' (2 Tim. 1:15–17, RSV)

How we would love to know a bit more about Onesiphorus! The New Testament is silent, but a mid second-century work, *The Acts of Paul and Thecla*, says he was a citizen of Iconium who, along with his wife Lectra, entertained Paul on his first missionary journey, and was converted through him. At all events, he had a household and a residence in Ephesus, and, like many of the wealthy merchants of the day, made occasional visits to Rome. On one of them he heard of Paul's imprisonment and made diligent – and successful – efforts to track him down. What a lot it must have meant to Paul to receive a visit like that from a trusted friend: prison can be not only lonely but dispiriting.

And Paul is still basking in the joy and encouragement of that visit as he writes to Timothy at Ephesus. There is no need to suppose that because his household is mentioned here Onesiphorus had died. He was clearly a man whose work often took him from home. Maybe he was still in Rome. At all events, Paul wants to show his gratitude for the visit by praying God's richest blessing upon the household from which it came. Here is an important example of praying not only for those who have helped them, but for the whole social milieu to which they belong: we are all influenced very much by our family situation, and it is great to know that friends who love us are praying about that.

Onesiphorus himself is not forgotten; far from it. But instead of simply lifting him to God in gratitude, as one of us might, Paul does something much more important. He prays that the whole lifestyle of Onesiphorus may be so Christlike that when he, in turn, comes to face death (Paul was at this moment very much contemplating his own, 4:6*ff*.) he will be able confidently to look up to the Lord for his mercy. 'Mercy' and 'the Day' are prominent in this letter. It would be good if we pleasure-loving, complacent twentieth-century Christians took both more seriously. One day we shall die. And then above all else we shall stand in need of the sheer unmerited mercy of the Lord. How wonderful when a Christian friend, like Paul, has the insight and the directness to pray for just that.

An enemy

The second letter to Timothy is rich in personal

petition by the apostle. At its conclusion we find him praying for a man called Alexander.

> 'Alexander the metalworker did me a great deal of harm. The Lord will repay him for what he has done. You too should be on your guard against him, because he strongly opposed our message. At my first defence, no-one came to my support, but everyone deserted me. May it not be held against them. But the Lord stood at my side and gave me strength . . .' (2 Tim. 4:14*ff.*).

What Alexander did to harm Paul we may never know. In all probability he was a leader in one of the metal-working guilds who were so angered by Paul's preaching against idolatry, and therefore against their business! We find that kind of feeling exploding at Ephesus a few years earlier in the famous scene sketched so brilliantly by Luke in Acts 19. At all events, Paul had found him a very dangerous opponent.

Some of the manuscripts read, 'may the Lord repay him according to his deeds'. But the better manuscripts make it a solemn statement of fact: 'the Lord will repay him'. We can leave vengeance to the Lord because he will repay, at his time, in his way, with his justice (Rom. 12:19). So here is not, in all probability, a prayer for retribution, but a statement of the awesome fact that God will judge one day, and we can safely leave our wrongs with the one who is incorruptible Justice and perfect Love. Paul's own forgiving attitude to those who have wronged him is clearly seen in verse 16: 'may it not be charged against them!'

A colleague

We have a marvellous example of Paul's prayer for a fellow Christian in the little letter to Philemon. Philemon was a wealthy landowner, living at, or just outside, Colossae, and Paul wrote to him by the same messenger, Tychicus, who delivered the Colossian letter. The situation was picaresque. Paul had himself brought Philemon to faith in Jesus some time earlier. One of Philemon's slaves, Onesimus, had subsequently run away, after stealing a lot of money, and eventually landed up (in the irony of God) in the same prison as Paul! Needless to say, Paul brings him, too, to Christ, and then together they address the difficult issue of what Onesimus should do to put things right after his release. They decide on a plan unthinkable for those times: Onesimus should go and give himself up, and Philemon should be asked to have him back no longer as a slave but as a brother Christian! Such is the revolutionary power of the gospel, even in the most heavily structured social situations. But once again Paul prefaces action by prayer. Here it is.

For Individuals

'I thank my God always when I remember you in my prayers, because I hear of your love and the faith which you have toward the Lord Jesus and all the saints, and I pray that the sharing of your faith may promote the knowledge of all the good that is ours in Christ' (Philemon vv. 4–6, RSV).

Once again we have the theme of remembering in prayer. Once again the gratitude for all that the Lord has done already in building his love and faith into Philemon's character. Once again the emphasis that real love towards Jesus must show itself by equally real love towards others. But what does Paul actually seek, in his prayer for his colleague?

If we are to follow the RSV and NIV it is a prayer for energy and effectiveness in outreach. He wants Philemon and his family, Apphia and Archippus, to spread the faith for all they are worth, so that others around them may know all the good things that are ours in Christ. That is a perfectly possible translation. It is an eminently Pauline emphasis. But it does not make much sense of the very delicate situation between Onesimus and Philemon which Paul is seeking to defuse. We should probably translate the original as follows: 'I pray that your fellowship with us in the common faith may become powerful in understanding all the blessings which are ours through union with

Christ.' Fellowship, *koinonia*, is the key word not only in this particular case, but in all transactions between fellow believers. We share a common Lord, a common faith, common 'good things' or blessings. And here Paul is trusting that the strength of that common faith and love which unite himself and Philemon in Christ, will be powerful enough to embrace a runaway slave who has also found the same faith and love in Jesus. There was a real danger that Philemon might do the normal thing to an escaped slave when recaptured: crucify him. Paul longs for him to set the man free, but in this most subtle and delicate letter he refrains from specifically asking that. Instead he prefers to pray that their common trust in the liberating grace of the Lord Jesus, and deep insight into all the good things he wants for his followers, will be so strong in Philemon that he comes to view Onesimus in the same way that Paul sees him, understanding that before God we are all Onesimuses!

What a way to pray for colleagues! Sometimes we have hard things to ask them, and are wondering if we should. Sometimes they are in difficult circumstances and do not know themselves what they should do. Fellowship is the key. We need to revel in that joint participation in Christ which both we and they possess, and to pray that this may be so strong in them that God will be able to guide them with great clarity towards what they should do. How

much better than praying in a rather horizontal
way, that what *we* think is best for them to do
should be carried out. Paul is concerned that what
Jesus thinks best should emerge, and so he prays
that Philemon should be as close to Jesus as he,
himself, is; and in consequence become very sure
of God's will. Of one thing he is certain. The Lord's
will is bound to be for 'the good'; it will lead us
further into recognising all the blessings that our
union with Christ brings.

Just four examples of Paul at prayer for individuals. But each one is full of suggestions and
encouragement.

For the Wider Church

8

For the Wider Church

We have just listened in to Paul praying for some individuals. Now we find him praying for Christians at large. This may not be altogether obvious, because we find his prayer in the first chapter of Ephesians, which looks as if it was directed to one specific church. This is, however, probably not the case.

For one thing, 'in Ephesus' in the salutation (Eph. 1:1) is missing from a number of manuscripts. If so, the text would read 'Paul, an apostle of Christ Jesus by the will of God, to the saints who are also faithful in Christ Jesus. . . .' For another reason, we are told that this was known in some circles as the Letter to the Laodiceans. Furthermore, when we recall that Paul spent three years of concentrated ministry in Ephesus, it is passing strange that this letter should have no reference either to the work there or to individuals in the church, if it was designed for Ephesus alone. No, much the best way to regard

Ephesians, is as a companion piece to Colossians, written by Paul in prison at the same time, and conveyed by the same messenger, Tychicus. It deals with the same great themes as Colossians, but it is devoid of any anti-heretical medicine, and we can imagine that it went indeed to Ephesus, but also to cities like Miletus, Laodicea and various others in the western part of the Province of Asia. It is designed to show the origin and development of the church of Christ which was beginning to be established worldwide, and to display to those who lived under the shadow of many an ancient pagan temple the unity and beauty of that more glorious temple of which Jesus is the chief cornerstone, and where Christians are stones in the superstructure.

How, then, does Paul pray for Ephesus and the cities around it? How does he pray for Christians as they begin to become a real factor across the world? Well, it is a marvellous, meditative prayer. The apostle may have been chained in a dungeon, but he had his head in heaven as he prayed, and as Tychicus scrambled to take notes. But the extended, meditative prayer does seem to fall into three clear sections. The first is heartfelt, unambiguous praise.

Paul's praise

'Blessed be the God and Father of our Lord Jesus
Christ, who has blessed us in Christ with every
spiritual blessing in the heavenly places, even
as he chose us in him before the foundation of
the world, that we should be holy and blameless
before him. He destined us in love to be his sons
through Jesus Christ, according to the purpose
of his will, to the praise of his glorious grace
which he freely bestowed on us in the Beloved.
In him we have redemption through his blood,
the forgiveness of our trespasses, according to
the riches of his grace which he lavished upon
us. For he has made known to us in all wisdom
and insight the mystery of his will, according to
his purpose which he set forth in Christ as a plan
for the fulness of time, to unite all things in him,
things in heaven and things on earth.

In him, according to the purpose of him who
accomplishes all things according to the counsel of his will, we who first hoped in Christ
have been destined and appointed to live for
the praise of his glory. In him you also, who
have heard the word of truth, the gospel of
your salvation, and have believed in him, were
sealed with the promised Holy Spirit, which is
the guarantee of our inheritance until we acquire

possession of it, to the praise of his glory' (Eph. 1:3–14, RSV).

If that all seems a bit breathless and 'over the top', *it is*! It is all one sentence in the original Greek. We are privileged to overhear a saint of God pouring out his heart in praise for the undreamed-of generosity of God's good news which has made new men and women of people all over the Roman Empire – and still does throughout the world today. Until we ourselves have some experience of becoming lost in wonder, love and praise, we shall not progress very far in the school of prayer.

It is impossible here to begin to expound so rich and deep a passage. But certain things stand out. To me, one of the most remarkable is the way in which the praise is centred upon God himself. It starts 'Blessed be God ... who has blessed us ... with every spiritual blessing'. In the New Testament God alone is addressed as 'Blessed'. Men are blessed when they receive his blessings: God is blessed when men receive his generosity with love and thankfulness. Three times 'blessing' is mentioned in that opening verse. Three times the passage insists that we are to live 'to the praise of his glory'. The reciprocity of his generosity and our responsive lifestyle could hardly be more clearly stated.

But suppose we feel like saying 'Come clean,

Paul. What does all this churchy language about God blessing us add up to? What does it mean?' The apostle has his reply ready, and he outlines a sevenfold blessing which God has poured out on all Christians the world over, and for which he wants to give God the glory and the praise that are his due.

i) *God has blessed us* (verse 3) with all spiritual blessings, which lie wrapped up, so to speak, in Christ. The author of this generosity is God. We are the recipients. The means by which we get them is 'in Christ' – they do not come to us piecemeal without our making room for him in our lives. The wealth of those blessings is incalculable: 'all'. The nature of these blessings is spiritual as opposed to the material wealth which often marked God's goodness in Old Testament times. And the time at which they became available was at our first connexion with Christ, when we 'received him' or were 'baptised into him': he *has* blessed us with them all. It is up to us to draw upon the blessings in Christ of which we are only dimly aware. What an astounding thought! All the blessings God intends for us are latent in the Christ with whom all Christians are already connected. There is no second (or hundredth!) blessing which can be added on top of him. They all simply make real in our experience what God intended for us when we first became

Christians! No wonder Paul is almost tongue-tied in praise.

He proceeds to unfold the nature of some of those blessings in verses 4–14 which follow. Three great themes are interwoven: 'in Christ' comes 12 times in 14 verses; 'according to the purpose of his will' comes three times in verses 5, 9 and 11; while 'to the praise of his glory' recurs in verses 6, 12 and 14. Respectively they denote the nature, the origin and the purpose of our lives.

ii) *God has chosen us*, destined us (verses 4, 5). What an encouragement that is. To be sure, we chose him. But with the benefit of hindsight we can see that he set his love upon us and chose us long before we were ever in the position to respond. Paul goes on to reflect on the reasons why God chose us: that we should be 'blameless' – with nothing held against us; that we should be 'holy' – his people; and that we should be 'before him . . . in love'. Then indeed we shall be to the praise of his glory. And Paul exults in the vision and generosity of such a God.

iii) *God has adopted us* (verse 5). It is as if we were street kids with a criminal record: and God in his love not only paid our fines and cleared our names, but adopted us into his own family alongside his one and only Son. What love that bespeaks! What confidence and freedom that gives! He has chosen us, even us, to be in his family.

iv) *God has rescued us* (verse 7) from the accusing load of our wrongdoings. What an evocative word, 'redemption'. To the Hebrew it would have meant rescue from guilt and alienation from God through a blood sacrifice. To the Greek it would have brought to mind mental images of slaves being set free from bondage after they had been bought, maybe, by a new master. That freeing from the guilt and the slavery of evil was immensely costly. It cost our Lord no less than 'the forgiveness of our trespasses', and that was achieved 'through his blood' on the cross. The cross of Christ takes us to the very heart of God and causes the angels to bow their heads in adoration.

v) *God has enlightened us* (verses 8, 9). Jesus Christ, in whom we are incorporated, is the key to life, to reality, to the whole universe. All will, one day, find its goal and fulfilment in him, the cosmic Christ. He is 'the steward of the fulness of the times' (v.10, Greek) and he will bring all that is in heaven and all that is on earth into a final harmony. It is impossible for us to imagine how this can be, or even what it could mean: but then it would have been no less impossible for us to conceive of Jew and Gentile being united in a single 'body of Christ', or graceless rebels being reconciled with a spotless, holy God. Both have come about through Christ. That gives us great confidence that at the end of all things he will indeed have the final, reconciling word.

vi) *God has acquired us* (verse 11). The God who works all things after the purpose of his own will destined us – yes, we know that! But Paul has a surprise for us. He destined us as his 'lot', his 'inheritance' (*klēros*). The God who fashioned the universe wants only this for his inheritance – the total loyalty and loving response of reconciled sinners like us! It would be marvellous enough to think that we have God for our inheritance, considering how worked up we get about what Aunt Matilda leaves us – or does not leave us – in her will. But that is, in all probability, not what is uppermost in the apostle's mind. He is awestruck with the thought that not only is God our inheritance: *we are God's*! The question for us, I suppose, is this: 'Is he enjoying his inheritance? Or are we robbing him?'

This is our God. This is his great design. He knew what he was doing. He planned it 'according to the counsel of his will'. He has the power to bring it about – for 'he accomplishes everything'. Praise God! We shall indeed, one day, be 'for the praise of his glory'.

vii) *God has sealed us* with his Holy Spirit (verse 13). The Holy Spirit, promised long ago in Joel and Ezekiel, has been graciously distributed, ever since Pentecost, to all members of the Lord's family, all

who have 'heard the word of truth, the gospel of
salvation' and have 'hoped in Christ'. Paul sees the
Spirit as having two special functions.

First, he is a 'seal'. And the seal is always, in
antiquity, the mark of ownership. You sealed your
letter with your personal stamp. You sealed your
belongings likewise. You even sealed your sheep
with a special branding iron. You intended others
to know who owned them. And it is like that
with God. He gives us his Holy Spirit so that it
should be obvious to all and sundry that there is
something different about us. We are his property,
his possession.

The other word the apostle uses here, 'guarantee', is no less significant. The Spirit is seen
as a 'down payment', a 'first instalment' of all
God's future blessings for us. We do not have
everything God is planning for us, yet. But we do
have the pledge, the guarantee, the first instalment
of God's future in the Holy Spirit who lives within
us. Heaven lies beyond our vision, but a little bit
of heaven is inside our hearts, the Holy Spirit. He
is the proof that the Lord will come back one day
to claim his own. The Spirit is the supremely real
first instalment of good things to come. It is hardly
surprising that in Modern Greek the word here
used, *arrhabōn*, means engagement ring, the pledge
of a blissful future. No wonder Paul ends once again
with awestruck love, 'to the praise of his glory'.

If there is anything this first part of Paul's amazing prayer in Ephesians chapter 1 teaches us, it is the prime importance of praise. Let us give priority to praising God. It is one of the clearest evidences of being sealed by the Spirit of God. And it is the only proper response of creatures before their Creator, and of ransomed sinners before their Saviour. Praise the Lord!

At last this extended time of praise leads into petition. Like the praise and the grounds which underlie it, this petition is applicable to everyone. It is literally worldwide. It is marvellous to use for believers anywhere.

Paul's Prayer

'For this reason, because I have heard of your faith in the Lord Jesus and your love toward all the saints, I do not cease to give thanks for you, remembering you in my prayers, that the God of our Lord Jesus Christ, the Father of glory, may give you a spirit of wisdom and of revelation in the knowledge of him, having the eyes of your hearts enlightened, that you may know what is the hope to which he has called you, what are the riches of his glorious inheritance in the saints, and what is the immeasurable greatness of his

power in us who believe, according to the working
of his great might which he accomplished in
Christ when he raised him from the dead . . .'
(Eph. 1:15–20a, RSV)

'For this reason', he begins! Knowing you are
God's heirs, knowing you belong, knowing he set
his love on you long before you ever responded,
knowing you believe, knowing you are destined for
his heavenly home – it is time to pray! 'Faith in
Jesus' and 'love toward all the saints' is a very
passable description of the authentic Christian life.
And so Paul launches into petition for his readers,
so that they may become what in God's purpose
they already are.

'Praising and remembering', he says. Not a long
prayer after all that praise, but very profound.
Notice what he asks. Not for things, but for people:
not for possessions, but for character. The cry of his
heart is 'Lord, make them understand'.

Understand what?

Paul is afraid that they have buried treasure in
their garden, barrels and barrels of the choicest
food, but they do not know it, and they survive
on husks. So he asks for wisdom, for perception,
for deep knowledge (*epignosis*) of Jesus, so that the
eyes of their hearts might be enlightened. Notice
that he does not say 'the eyes of their minds'. It

is all too possible to have the most immaculate theological insights and yet be blind to the realities of what the Lord offers us. It is not only our minds that need his touch, it is our blind hearts.

What, then, does he long to see them understand?

First, the hope of God's calling. The call is in the past, and they have responded to it. But what they hope for lies in the future, and they have not yet attained it. The call of God brings to people without hope (Eph. 2:12) a confident assurance of a future dominated by God himself. Nor is this 'pie in the sky when you die'. It is something we can be sure about because of the presence of the Holy Spirit in our hearts here and now. Confidence in that future should have a profound shaping effect upon our lives. Paul would agree with John's words on the matter: 'See what love the Father has given us, that we should be called children of God; and so we are. . . . Beloved, we are God's children now; it does not yet appear what we shall be, but we know that when he appears we shall be like him, for we shall see him as he is. And everyone who thus hopes in him purifies himself as he is pure' (1 John 3:1–3, RSV).

Second, the wealth of God's inheritance. Paul is dreaming of God's inheritance, which he gives to us Christians (his 'glorious inheritance among the saints'). It is something we come to appreciate corporately, not in isolation. It is something which we only gradually understand, as our eyes might slowly adjust to a brilliant sunlit landscape after being imprisoned in a gloomy cave for years. As we are enlightened by the Holy Spirit, who is himself the first instalment of that inheritance, we gradually come to see more and more of the wonder of what God has invited us to share: the greatest and most satisfying inheritance in all the world. It is nothing less than the inheritance of God himself, which Christians share with his Son Jesus Christ. There is nothing starry-eyed about all this: Paul knows well that suffering is an inescapable part of our lot, as it was of Christ's. He is no less sure that glory lies at the end of the road. 'We are children of God, and if children, then heirs, heirs of God and fellow heirs with Christ, provided we suffer with him in order that we may also be glorified with him. I consider that the sufferings of this present time are not worth comparing with the glory that is to be revealed to us' (Rom. 8:16–18, RSV).

What better could one pray for friends in Christ than that they might grow in appreciation of their inheritance in him, and might come to enter more and more fully into all that God has in store for them?

Third, the greatness of God's power. The power of God is the great present reality we need to come to terms with, fulfilling the past calling and leading on to the future inheritance. Once again Paul leaves us speechless with his prayer. What does he pray that they may know?

God's power? No!

The greatness of his power? No!

The surpassing nature of the greatness of his power? No!

None of that will match up to what Paul longs for his readers. His heart's desire is that they may know nothing less than the power of the resurrection itself in their lives! The power he prays for (with a rush of almost ungrammatical words) is 'in line with (*kata*) the energy of the power of his might which he wrought in Christ when he raised him from the dead.' That is what we are talking about. Supernatural power. Power beyond anything we human beings could attain to by our unaided efforts. The very power of God himself, the power which raised Christ from the tomb on the first Easter day.

How about that? What a thing to realise in our own lives. What a thing to pray for our friends. So often we trudge around with our eyes on the ground and little expectation of help from God – when all the time the power of the resurrection is waiting to be unleashed in us if only we make the connection of prayer!

I recall once reading of a very heavily laden tanker which sank, years ago, at the mouth of New York harbour. Strenuous efforts were made to shift it, but without avail. The tugs could not move it from the bottom. And then someone had a brilliant idea: to fix steel cables tight around it at low tide, and wait for the tide to do what the tugs could not! It was highly effective. The efforts of even the strongest of us are as ineffective as those tugs in changing habits and attitudes, and dealing with inner hurts in our lives: but if only we allow these things to be linked up with the boundless power of the tide, the tide of God which swept Jesus up from that cold grave on the first Easter, we shall know in our own experience the very thing for which Paul prayed, and which he so clearly exhibited in his own life: the power of the resurrection.

That is what Paul prayed for the church universal. Just three things, but if they are present, this life will prove to be the ante-chamber of heaven.

But remember, we broke off in the midst of a sentence when we looked at Paul's petition. And that is significant: for this man had learnt to let his prayers move into adoration and pure worship of the living God.

Paul's contemplation

'And that you may know ... his great might which he accomplished in Christ when he raised him from the dead and made him sit at his right

139

hand in the heavenly places, far above all rule and authority and power and dominion, and above every name that is named, not only in this age but also in that which is to come; and he has put all things under his feet and has made him the head over all things for the church, which is his body, the fulness of him who fills all in all' (Eph. 1:20–23, RSV).

As he lies in his prison, all thoughts of those he has been praying for fade away. Paul is caught up with Christ in God. He has no eyes for any, except Jesus only, the one whom God raised in vindication of his claims and his achievements; Jesus who is now accorded by God the Father the highest honour in the cosmos. Paul is totally taken up with his Beloved. And that is the nature of true contemplation.

He sees his Jesus as *crowned king*. God has 'set him at his own right hand in the heavenly places', and this of course fulfils the vision of Psalm 110:1, a verse often referred to in the New Testament. The exaltation of the king of Israel as God's anointed lent itself very naturally to the exaltation of Jesus after his work on earth was accomplished. 'The LORD says to my Lord: "Sit at my right hand, till I make your enemies your footstool."' Jesus is exalted on high, and Paul bows in wonder at his feet.

He sees Jesus as *ultimate victor*. He is 'far above all rule and authority and power and dominion and above every name that is named, not only in this age but also in that which is to come'. Paul is clearly alluding here to the views of men called Gnostics who thought of a kind of ladder of intermediary powers between the material world on the one hand and God on the other. He never bothers to speculate about such powers, though he is well aware of unseen spiritual forces of darkness (*cf.* Col. 2:15, Eph. 6:12). He simply asserts, with sublime confidence on the ground of the cross and resurrection, that Jesus is the ultimate victor over all of them. His is the name above every name, and at the End all will have to bow to it and confess that Jesus is Lord, to the glory of God the Father (Phil. 2:11). Paul needs no bidding to bow and confess Christ's Lordship now!

He sees Jesus as *perfect man*. His mind goes to Psalm 8, where the psalmist wonders:

'When I look at thy heavens, the work of thy fingers, the moon and the stars which thou hast established; what is man that thou art mindful of him, and the son of man that thou dost care for him? Yet thou hast made him little less than God, and dost crown him with glory and honour. Thou hast given him dominion over the works of thy hands; thou hast

141

put all things under his feet' (Psalm 8:3–6, RSV).

That is what man was intended to be, the glorious crown of God's creation, living in total dependence on God and obedience to him. But man has proved unequal to this high calling and has fallen into sinful rebellion. Not so Jesus! In him Paul sees the perfect obedience to God and the perfect sovereignty over the world to which mankind was given dominion. His eyes are on the Perfect Man, and he longs progressively to be transformed, along with his readers, into the likeness of that Perfect Man.

Finally, he sees Jesus as *head of the church*. The church is 'the body'. Jesus is 'the head'. The head which is the source of life. The head which is the organ of sovereignty. The head which is the direction-giver to the whole body. The church is indissolubly linked with this exalted head. It is called to unconditional obedience to his every wish. It is meant to be the expression of his invisible presence. It is meant to be the recipient of the fulness which he constantly longs to pour into his body and every limb in it. And in a final act of daring, Paul sees the church as something which brings fulness to Christ himself – for this is how the Greek is best construed. In some mysterious way the head has determined to be incomplete without the body. There is a profound interdependence between the church and its Lord.

This is the Jesus who fills Paul's gaze as he prays for the worldwide church of God. He is the Alpha and the Omega of all existence, and prayer properly brings us to his feet in utter awe and wonder as we contemplate his glory.

In Meditation

9

In Meditation

The prayer in chapter 1 of Ephesians sprang from praise. The prayer in chapter 3:14–21 emerges from meditation. He began it in verse 1 of the chapter, 'For this reason I, Paul, a prisoner for Christ Jesus on behalf of you Gentiles –', and then he got distracted by the wonder of the gospel reaching the Gentiles. The next 12 verses are a meditation on this theme, and then Paul returns to where he left off. 'For this reason I bow my knees before the Father . . .'

There is nothing wrong with having distractions in our prayers. Of course we must not court them. That is why Jesus told us to go into our room and shut the door when we pray. But distractions will come whether the door is closed or not! And the best way I find to handle them is not to fight them but to follow them, and turn them into meditation before God or possibly into intercession to him. That is what Paul does here. His digression about the

147

Gentiles is extremely fruitful; the same can be said of our digressions and wandering thoughts in prayer. After all, the Lord may want us to go down that particular side alley!

The meditation

This, I fancy, was a meditation which St Paul never intended, as he lay in prison dictating his letter to the Ephesians – and others. But as he mentioned the word 'Gentiles' he stopped in his tracks, and began to marvel at the way his life had turned out. He had been the strictest type of Jew, unwilling even to spit at 'Gentile dogs', lest his spit be defiled! Yet God had reached him with the gospel which he strove so hard to suppress. And in the course of the succeeding years, it was borne in upon him that he, Paul, was to be a prime instrument of God to reach those very same Gentiles whom he had once despised – and reach them with this gospel which he had once tried to destroy. As he looks back, he marvels at the gospel itself, the very mystery of Christ. In previous generations this mystery had lain unknown, although prophets had hinted at it. But now what was once hidden is bathed in glorious light: the Gentiles, the outsiders, are to be fellow-heirs with God's chosen people the Jews, and partners in the same promises that were made centuries earlier to Abraham and his descendants.

Paul marvels at the birth of a new race, where words like 'Jew' and 'Gentile', so terribly divisive, cease to have meaning. The new day has come. The church has been born!

And as he turns over in his chains, he cannot help reflecting on the irony of it, that he, the pupil of Gamaliel, the super-orthodox Jew, should have been chosen by God to make this glorious message of new life, new unity, known to the once despised Gentiles. But more than the irony, the shame of the situation bit deep into his soul. He was 'the very least of all saints'. In his agitation he coins a word, making a comparative out of a superlative: 'I am less than the least of all Christians'. Is this mock humility, hyperbole? No. For he is so painfully aware of the years of hatred in his heart against Jesus and all that he stood for; of those violent excursions when he had gone out to capture and kill the followers of this Way. And now it was he who was in prison, and the message had spread everywhere throughout the world! This was the eternal purpose of the Lord himself, he reflects. More, the union of Jew and Gentile, those age-long irreconcilables, in one church fellowship was something which showed the 'many-coloured' wisdom of God to the principalities and powers in the heavenly places. The angels (if it is they and not the evil powers that he means) are confronted by something that they simply have no experience of: the reconciling grace of God that brings Jew and non Jew alike to the throne of his mercy and unites them in one body. That is a mighty theme. So there is no need for the readers to lose heart, if they are scattered, lonely, facing hardship or persecution. They are on the victory side. They are part of God's master plan. And so is Paul. They do not need to grieve for him, although he is in prison. On the contrary, author and readers alike should make good use of their boldness and confidence of access to God through Jesus Christ, and pour out their hearts before him in prayer. And that is precisely what Paul himself goes on to do.

A wonderful meditation, this: and one which greatly enriches his prayer which follows.

The prayer

'For this reason I bow my knees before the Father, from whom every family in heaven and on earth is named, that according to the riches of his glory he may grant you to be strengthened with might through his Spirit in the inner man, and that Christ may dwell in your hearts through faith; that you, being rooted and grounded in love, may have power to comprehend with all the saints what is the breadth and length and height and depth, and to know the love of Christ which surpasses knowledge, that you may be filled with all the fulness of God' (Eph. 3:14–19, RSV).

How does he pray?

His chains allow the apostle to kneel as he prays. Jews did not always kneel. Often they stood. Sometimes they sat, or lay prostrate. But there is something very fitting about the kneeling position in prayer. It is so reverent. It makes the respective positions of God and ourselves so plain. It is good for us to kneel.

And he prays with a deep concern for these Gentiles over whom he has been brooding. Urgency in prayer comes from his time of meditation. As he sees the wonder of what God has delighted to do in them, he is deeply concerned that they should not fail to be the salt and the light in the world that God intended.

This prayer, too, is permeated by a sense of wonder at being in God's family. How could God have bothered to reach out to estranged Gentiles like them, and proud Jews like him with the gospel? Yet he had, and had brought them both into the same divine family. It is a wonderful launch-pad for prayer.

Notice, too, how as so often in his prayers, Paul makes love his aim. Love is the language of heaven itself, and unless it is seen in the lives of Christians, nobody will be attracted to the Saviour.

And, as we shall see in a moment, Paul's prayer ends with a marvellous ascription of glory to the God who is well able to do what he asks. His petition culminates in adoration.

To whom does he pray?

He prays to 'the Father'. In his pre-Christian days he could never have addressed the High and Holy One who inhabits eternity in such a fashion. But Jesus had given to his followers the unspeakable privilege of addressing God in the same way as he himself did, calling him 'Abba, dear Daddy'. Did not the Lord's Prayer begin 'When you pray, say *Abba* . . . ?' That word takes us to the very heart of God. He is no cruel tyrant, no absent despot, but a loving Father, a dear Daddy. 'Daddy' to Jesus – and Jesus alone, in the full sense of the word. But Daddy, too, in a derived sense, to those who are adopted alongside Jesus as children in the family. 'And because you are sons,' Paul had written a few years earlier, 'God has sent the Spirit of his Son into our hearts, crying "Abba! Father!" So through God you are no longer a slave but a son, and if a son then an heir' (Galatians 4:6–7, RSV). What a ground from which to start praying!

But Paul does not leave it there. He reflects a little more on the Father to whom he is about to pray. 'All fatherhood in heaven and earth springs from him.' If you like, 'any father-headed group'

in heaven or earth derives from him. One of the
ancient commentators put it beautifully: 'The name
of father did not go up from us, but from above it
came to us.' Incidentally, what a contrast to the
ideas of Freud. His dealing with mentally-ill people
persuaded him that God was a projection into the
untenanted heavens of our own father-image. I do
not know many people who would want their 'old
man' as God! But Paul tells us something very
different: that our human family relations, spoiled
and marred as they are by sin and discord, are
nevertheless pale reflections of that perfect Parent
in heaven who is the ultimate source of all love
and all families. I can pray with confidence to
such a God! So could the scattered groups of
Christians throughout Asia Minor, often weak,
sometimes persecuted, frequently discouraged, to
whom Paul writes, and whom he encourages not to
lose heart but to make use of their right of access
to the Father.

What does he pray for?

First, he prays for strength through the Spirit. He
wants them to be mightily strengthened. And he
adds a delightful touch. He wants it to be not 'out
of' the Father's riches, but 'according to' them. If
a Rockefeller or a Howard Hughes gave us ten
pounds, it would certainly come out of his riches,
but it would scarcely be 'according to' them. God

153

does not give us the strength of his Holy Spirit in any stingy way. The gift is overwhelming, like the love and the riches of the Giver.

Secondly, he prays that Christ may dwell in their hearts through faith. And that is no unnecessary prayer for churchmen throughout the world. It is all too possible to go to church for years without ever having welcomed Christ into the heart. Far too many churchpeople think Christianity is something we do for God, rather than allowing him to come and minister to us. They think it is a matter of doing good and religious things: instead, it begins with receiving a gracious, indwelling, Saviour. I recall preaching on this passage once, in a very respectable (and very dour) church. It happened to be the set reading for the day. As I explained what it meant, some people came up to me afterwards with tears in their eyes saying they had been thirsting for a message such as this for years in that church: others were very angry to hear that it was possible to be a churchman but never to have made room for the church's Lord and Master in your heart. Paul knew that well. That is why he prayed that his readers would not be 'paper Christians', but people who had genuinely put their trust in Jesus and asked him to come and make his home in their lives.

And that is precisely what the Greek word translated 'dwell' means. It means 'be at home'. There is another, rather similar word which means 'be a temporary resident'. But that is not what Paul is after. He wants Christians who have not only welcomed Christ into their lives but who have made him at home. There is no aspect of their lives he may not inspect. There is no place in their lives he may not go. Christians like that are going to be some use in the world!

Thirdly, Paul prays for love in their experience. You cannot have Christ in your heart without having love on board. But just as Paul wants Jesus to be at home in their lives, so he wants the love of Jesus to flow all over and through them. From love to love. That is the progression of the Christian life. We are meant to be grounded in it and growing in it. There is no higher thing to pray for anyone, than that they may grow in the love of God. For love is the language of heaven. It is the very nature of the Trinity.

And because the God we worship is unity in plurality, the experience of Christian love is of the same kind. It is not in lonely cultivation of our souls but 'with all the saints' that we begin to grasp the love of God which defies language. Paul has a lovely word for it, derived from the hunting field: the love of God is something which no hound can track! But it is real all the same. We see it in some people. We feel it when we are in their presence. And God wants his children to emanate that warmth and

light of love. But we can't give it out until we take
it in, and the apostle prays that his readers may
have the strength to do just that, and comprehend
the breadth and length and height and depth of the
love of Jesus which has loved them into life.

What does Paul mean by these dimensions? Probably he is simply drawing attention to the diverse
ways in which true love shows itself. But if we
were to press him he might not mind! The *length*
of the love of God, the length it is willing to go, is
limitless: 'He is able to save for all time those who
draw near to God through him, since he always
lives to make intercession for them' (Heb. 7:25,
RSV). The *breadth* of God's love is shown by the
fact that Jesus Christ is 'the expiation for our sins,
and not for ours only, but also for the sins of the
whole world' (1 John 2:2, RSV). And what of the
depth of the love of Christ? 'You know the grace
of our Lord Jesus Christ, that though he was rich,
yet for your sake he became poor, so that by his
poverty you might become rich' (2 Cor. 8:9, RSV).
And the *height* of it? Well, 'God, who is rich in
mercy, out of the great love with which he loved us,
even when we were dead through our trespasses,
made us alive together with Christ . . . and raised
us up with him, and made us sit with him in the
heavenly places . . .' (Eph. 2:4*ff*., RSV).

Such is the generosity of our Lord Jesus Christ.
May we make the Indweller so much at home in our

lives that his love will overflow into every corner. It will mean that we are 'filled with all the fulness of God' – and what is that, but love?

The conclusion

Paul ends this marvellous prayer with adoring commitment to the Lord to whom he prays.

> 'Now to him who by the power at work within us is able to do far more abundantly than all that we ask or think, to him be glory in the church and in Christ Jesus to all generations, for ever and ever, Amen' (Eph. 3:20–21, RSV).

Nobody has ever framed a bolder prayer than the one Paul has just prayed: that his readers be filled with all the fulness of God. And yet this apostle, who has the abiding power to surprise us, does it yet again: he triumphantly invokes a power which is able to do a great deal more than he asks.

These are words of adoring commitment by St Paul to his loving Lord.

Look, first, at the *promise he claims*.

God is able to do what we ask.

God is able to do what we ask or think.

God is able to do abundantly above what we ask or think.

God is able to do far more abundantly than all
that we can ask or think.

There is no limit to God's power. It soars above
all we can ask or even imagine. And here is this
prayer warrior in his filthy cell, utterly convinced
that nothing, no nothing, is too hard for his God.
That is the sort of faith that the living God delights
to answer. It does not only request, but exhibits 'the
power at work within us'.

Second, look at the *sequel he envisages*.

The climax and culmination of his prayer and
meditation is simple: it is that glory should accrue
to the God and Father of our Lord Jesus Christ for
ever. Glory to him in the church. Glory to him in the
Saviour. This is the goal of Paul's vision. God is all
in all, and his praise echoes throughout time and
eternity. At the furthest horizon of our imagination
we see Jesus and his people rendering to the Father
in heaven that unceasing glory and praise which is
his due.

What a man of prayer we find in Saul of Tarsus!
But he would not be interested in our admiration.
He would say to us as tersely as he did to the
Thessalonians:

Pray without ceasing!